D1129781

Combat Aircraft Library

# Modern American
# Combat
# Aircraft

David A. Anderton

**Hamlyn/Aerospace**

London • New York • Sydney • Toronto

Published by
The Hamlyn Publishing Group Limited
London • New York • Sydney • Toronto
Astronaut House, Hounslow Road, Feltham,
Middlesex, England

Produced by Stan Morse
Aerospace Publishing Ltd
10 Barley Mow Passage
London W4 4PH

© Copyright Aerospace Publishing Ltd 1982

Colour profiles and line drawings © Copyright Pilot Press Ltd

First published 1982

ISBN 0 600 35022 3

All rights reserved. No part of this publication may be reproduced, stored in a retrieval system,
or transmitted in any form or by any means, electronic, mechanical, photocopying, recording
or otherwise, without the prior permission of The Hamlyn Publishing Group Limited, Aerospace
Publishing Limited and the Copyright holders.

All correspondence concerning the content of this volume should be addressed to
Aerospace Publishing Limited. Trade enquiries should be addressed to The Hamlyn Publishing
Group Limited.

Printed in Italy

## PICTURE ACKNOWLEDGEMENTS

The publishers would like to thank the following people and organisations listed below for their
help in supplying photographs for this book.

**Jacket front:** Grumman. **Jacket back:** General Dynamics. **Page 1:** US Air Force. **4:** Fairchild
Corporation. **5:** Boeing. **6:** (top) US Army. **8:** General Dynamics. **9:** Bell Helicopter Textron.
**10:** Hughes/Boeing Vertol. **11:** US Army/Bell. **12:** Bell. **13:** Hughes/Hughes. **14:** Sikorsky/
Sikorsky. **15:** Grumman/US Air Force. **16:** Grumman. **17:** Lindsay Peacock. **18:** (bottom)
Lindsay Peacock. **19:** Grumman. **24:** Grumman/Grumman. **25:** Vought Corporation. **26:** US
Navy/US Navy. **27:** Lockheed Corporation. **28:** British Aerospace. **29:** Lockheed. **32:** McDonnell
Douglas. **34:** McDonnell Douglas/McDonnell Douglas. **35:** Bell/McDonnell Douglas. **36:**
Sikorsky/US Navy. **37:** Sikorsky/Sikorsky. **38:** US Air Force. **39:** Boeing/General Dynamics.
**44:** (top) General Dynamics. **45:** US Air Force/General Dynamics. **46:** Boeing/Rockwell
Corporation. **47:** Lindsay Peacock/Lindsay Peacock. **48:** McDonnell Douglas. **49:** McDonnell
Douglas/US Air Force. **58:** General Dynamics/General Dynamics. **59:** Fairchild/Fairchild.
**64:** McDonnell Douglas/Denis Calvert. **65:** Vought Corporation/Lockheed. **66:** US Air Force/
US Air Force. **67:** US Air Force. **68:** US Air Force. **69:** Grumman. **70:** US Air Force/
US Air Force. **71:** McDonnell Douglas. **72:** Grumman/Vought. **73:** US Air Force/Vought.
**74/75:** McDonnell Douglas. **76:** McDonnell Douglas. **77:** US Air Force/US Air Force.
**78:** Hughes/McDonnell Douglas. **79:** Vought. **80:** US Air Force.

# Foreword

If one could define 'modern combat', it would make life very much easier for airmen who write requirements and designers who plan new aircraft. Combat never turns out as foreseen, and so it forces new concepts of use upon someone's preconceived notion of the proper employment of a weapon.

Examples abound in military history. A recent one is the employment of Strategic Air Command's (SAC) Boeing B-52 Stratofortresses on most of their missions in the war in South East Asia. They were designed to be strategic bombers, capable of accurately dropping nuclear ordnance or other weapons on targets from level flight at high altitude. In that war, they first flew tactical missions in support of ground troops, a role for which they were never intended and in which, initially, they could only perform poorly. Not without reason were their arduous flights termed 'splinter missions'.

So as you read this book, be aware that the uses described are what designers and military planners thought they might be when the aircraft were in the design stages. Some of the intended employment will be biased by wartime experiences in South East Asia; others, by the expected nature of a battle between the Warsaw Pact nations and NATO over a European killing-ground. Should these aircraft ever again become involved in a war, it is a safe bet that they will be used in ways their designers never envisaged.

# Contents

# Introduction to Modern Air Combat

Today, the military scene is a complex multi-environment business with the world as its theatre. Submarines haunt the ocean depths and satellites patrol the heavens. But most envisaged battles will take place within the scope of aircraft, and air power is the key to military dominance and security.

This is dangerous ground to tread. Modern air combat is going to be defined by who fights, and where, not by a military historian sitting far from any site of prospective combat.

Too often air combat is treated as if it were primarily a contest between opposing fighter aircraft, high in the blue, with an occasional foray by strategic bombers. But this is not so: modern air combat pulls out all the stops and uses all the airborne weapons systems available. Further, it depends to an enormous extent on the clever and subtle use of the available spectrum of electro-magnetic radiation to monitor enemy communications, watch his movements, and help destroy his trucks, tanks and aircraft.

Modern air combat is the infrequent and inconclusive encounters between the airmen in the Iraqi/Iranian war and the Israeli attack on the Iraqi nuclear reactor site. It is a USAF Lockheed SR-71 'Blackbird' undetected above an Arctic peninsula, and a pair of red-starred Tupolev Tu-20 'Bears' escorted down the Atlantic coast of the United States. Modern air combat is ground-

*A pair of Fairchild A-10A Thunderbolt II tank-killers is readied for a sortie during an exercise in Germany.*

controlled interception of a strike force, and an anti-aircraft missile. It is US Army helicopters, USAF forward air controllers, US Navy fighter directors. It is, in short, a most complex stew of weapons, people, communications and supporting services.

Modern air combat, in this book and in the majority of 'real-world scenarios', is confined to a tactical war in a single theatre. In contrast strategic war is an all-out nuclear exchange that would involve the triad of US forces: SAC's B-52s and ICBMs, and the US Navy's submarine-launched ballistic missiles. Air combat would be relatively unimportant in strategic war, but is a fundamental form of conflict in tactical war.

## Tank assault through Europe

It is hardly any secret that the United States believes it ought to plan for a war between the Warsaw Pact nations and the NATO alliance (for which read United States). This war is, almost invariably, assumed to begin with a massive tank assault originating from the forests and hills of the German Democratic Republic (DDR) behind the Fulda Gap, a throughway to the West located less than 70 miles (113 km) north east of Frankfurt-am-Main. Hundreds, even thousands of Russian-built tanks grind through the Gap and head for the English Channel, hoping to bisect NATO in less than two weeks. With them come waves of tactical fighter-bombers, and a mobile defensive shield of anti-aircraft artillery and missiles.

Arrayed to stop them are the tripwire forces of NATO air and ground units. The NATO air strength is a conglomeration of European and American aircraft of varying capabilities, availability and performance. The plan is that these forces, employing armour, helicopters and tactical aircraft with weapons that can destroy armoured columns, will blunt the drive, pound it with fighter-bombers (perhaps using tactical nuclear weapons) and send it scuttling back for the border, tails between legs. Reinforcements from the United States and other NATO partners will strengthen the defensive line and switch to the offensive if the Pact countries try a second move.

The Fulda Gap scenario has been an obsession with air planners for years now. But recently, and particularly as the result of events in the Middle East, war-gamers have begun to broaden their outlook and to consider other areas of the world where trouble might erupt. One such spot is Korea, where the divided country is still unstable. Planners foresee a miniature Fulda Gap scenario, with Kim Il Sung's troops roaring out of the North in armoured columns, supported by a strong tactical air arm. They will be countered by the Republic of Korea air force and by American air and ground units stationed in that country. Again, rapid US reinforcements from Japanese and American bases will arrive to shore up the defence lines.

The third scenario currently in favour sees action in the Middle East, quite likely in the Persian Gulf. There, one of the problems being studied is a Russian air attack on the US 6th Fleet, an

*In this Boeing E-4B airborne command post, key government officials will survive the initial scourge of an atomic conflict. The rest of the nation will have it pretty bad; but they can die secure in the knowledge that their leaders live on . . . for what?*

# Introduction to Modern Air Combat

*When the US Army moves helicopters, it moves helicopters. This batch of assorted Hueys is parked in a holding area at Norfolk, Virginia, before being shipped to Europe for the 'Reforger' exercise in 1976.*

attempt to drive that segment of the surface US Navy from those waters. Such a confrontation would be very risky. The closeness of traditional enemies in that region, coupled with the massive military might deployed throughout the area, would make it almost a certainty that a single raid by a Russian squadron would escalate within hours to a full-fledged war in the region.

There are certain similarities between the Fulda Gap and the Korean scenarios; they both involve an armoured assault which must be stopped and then turned. That requires a disproportionate amount of tactical air power, armed with the latest in tank-killing ammunition and missiles. Strategic bombers would likely not be used in the Fulda Gap scenario, on the assumption that the Russians would see that as an unacceptable escalation leading to all-out nuclear exchange. But since North Korea poses a far smaller threat of that outcome, it is likely

*The idea of dropping retarded bombs from a B-52 would have seemed ludicrous 30 years ago, but today even the latest model, the fan-engined B-52H, has to operate at low level. At this level the maximum speed is just on 400 mph (644 kmh).*

*An assault by Cobra gunship helicopters is hardly a surprise to the enemy because characteristic rotor slap can be heard minutes beforehand. Most of this formation, launching rockets in Exercise 'Bright Star '82', are so-called Production AH-1S models with flat-plate canopies.*

*Though it is a jet, the Lockheed C-141B StarLifter is an efficient platform for a paratroop assault, seen here demonstrated in Exercise 'Bright Star '82' in Egypt. This mission would have been performed even better by the C-17, cancelled in early 1982.*

that the first tactical strikes against those Communist forces would be soon amplified by a B-52 strike against Pyongyang and other major cities in North Korea.

The Persian Gulf scenario involves US Navy fighters, directed to intercept the oncoming bombers and their air-to-surface missiles. Other US Navy aircraft would be launched for electronic warfare, for command and control purposes, and for support tasks. It is likely that such a Russian thrust would be accompanied by additional attacks by surface and sub-surface ships, and that American carrier aircraft would arm for anti-shipping strikes, while the surface ships screening the force, and their helicopters, would go after the submarines.

These scenarios, and others like them, are the driving forces behind today's requirements for modern combat aircraft. They define performance parameters, the armament to be carried, and the environmental conditions that will test the combined weapons systems. The Fulda Gap and the Korean war plans obviously influenced the design of the Fairchild Republic A-10A Thunderbolt II, an aircraft specifically developed to destroy the armoured vehicles available now

# Introduction to Modern Air Combat

to the Warsaw Pact countries. The Russian threat of a combined bomber and missile assault on carrier-based US Navy forces was a major consideration in the design and evolution of the Grumman F-14A Tomcat. The need for a versatile, and less-expensive, combat fighter that could handle assignments at high and low altitudes prompted both the US Air Force and the US Navy to sponsor development programmes. Out of the one came the General Dynamics F-16A Fighting Falcon, and from the other the McDonnell Douglas/Northrop F-18A Hornet.

What has made the difference to American designers of fighters and bombers alike is not the offensive weaponry available to them, but the defensive weapons available to prospective enemies. The absolutely overwhelming superiority of Warsaw Pact forces in anti-aircraft artillery and missiles has changed the face of air warfare and of aircraft design. It has been as influential on tactics and on weapon design as the employment of the machine-gun was during World War I. The Vietnam experience was, in effect, the tip of the iceberg. The North Vietnamese were able to deploy and operate simple anti-aircraft missiles with all the problems and crudities of first-generation weapons, and to seize temporary control of the air in selected areas and belts of altitude. The proliferation of those missiles and their later successors, and their augmentation by batteries of automatic, radar-directed anti-aircraft artillery, threaten to take control of the air away from their opponents.

## Air superiority the keystone

Control of the air is, to any airman, the single keystone of the whole structure of air power. Remove it, and the structure collapses. Without control of the air, no air force can maintain a defensive and protective umbrella over its brothers-in-arms on the surface. Without air superiority, clearly and cleanly defined, no ground troops and no surface navy can move confidently against an enemy. Without air superiority, no air force can send its tactical aircraft against the strong points that hinder friendly ground forces, or on the interdiction strikes that will destroy the enemy's accumulation of invasion wealth: the troops, reinforcements, reserves, supplies and equipment that lie in depth behind his forward lines of advance.

Many techniques and much equipment have been developed to give tactical aircraft a fighting chance against the enemy's in-depth defence of anti-aircraft artillery and missiles. Very low-level attacks, stand-off missiles, and the whole panoply of electronic-warfare deceits have helped, and will continue to help, in specific situations. New tactical jamming aircraft will make it difficult for an enemy missile site to use its guidance radars. New hunter-killer techniques will hit anti-aircraft weapons that depend on electronic emissions for direction. But the contest will be difficult and costly.

*For low drag some aircraft, such as the MiG-21, MiG-23 and the original Harrier, have a canopy flush with the top of the fuselage. To win in air combat one does better with a rear view, which you get from the F-16A even when lying in the semi-reclining seat. The F-16B (right) is just as good.*

# The Army's Air Strength

**Restrained in the kinds of fixed-wing air power it may deploy, the US Army does all right with helicopters—and with a diverse and sophisticated force of fixed-wing aircraft. It is still one of the world's biggest air forces, and it flies and fights where the ground action is.**

'What would we do without helicopters? We would be fighting a different war, for a smaller area, at a greater cost, with less effectiveness. We might as well have asked: "What would General Patton have done without his tanks?"'. This, from General William C. Westmoreland, then commander of the US Military Assistance Command, Vietnam, simply underscores the importance of the helicopter to today's United States Army.

The US Army's use of rotary-winged aircraft dates back to the Korean conflict, when they were first used by that service for medical evacuation and resupply. Time after time they proved their value in combat situations, at the forward edge of the battle area. They were welcome sights to the US Army foot soldier, who looked to the sky for ammunition, hot rations, medical supplies, and—if he were hit—quick and relatively painless movement to a rear area hospital.

But it was in the Vietnam war that the helicopter really came into its own in US Army use. Says the Department of the Army's *Tactical and Materiel Innovations*, one of a series of Vietnam Studies:

*Bell UH-1 'Huey' helicopters, loaded down with weapons and troops, were the backbone of the US Army's air mobility in Vietnam.*

# Bell AH-1 HueyCobra

**SPECIFICATION**
**Bell AH-1T TOWCobra**
**Type:** close-support armed helicopter
**Powerplant:** (AH-1J) one 1,800-shp (1342-kW) Pratt & Whitney Aircraft of Canada T400-CP-400 turboshaft; (AH-1T) one 1,970-shp (1469-kW) Pratt & Whitney Aircraft of Canada T400-WV-402 turboshaft
**Performance:** (AH-1J) maximum speed 207 mph (333 km/h); maximum range (no reserves) 359 miles (578 km)
**Weights:** (AH-1J) operating 7,261 lb (3294 kg); basic combat 9,972 lb (4523 kg); maximum take-off 10,000 lb (4536 kg); (AH-1T) empty 8,014 lb (3635 kg); operating 8,608 lb (3905 kg); maximum take-off 14,000 lb (6350 kg)
**Dimensions:** (AH-1J) main rotor diameter 44 ft 0 in (13.41 m), tail rotor diameter 8 ft 6 in (2.59 m), length (rotor turning) 52 ft 11½ in (16.14 m), height 13 ft 6¼ in (4.12 m), main rotor disc area 1,520 sq ft (141.25 m²); (AH-1T) main rotor diameter 48 ft 0 in (14.63 m), tail

rotor diameter 9 ft 8½ in (2.96 m), length (rotor turning) 58 ft 0 in (17.68 m), main rotor disc area 1,809.5 sq ft (168.11 m²)
**Armament:** (AH-1J) XM197 20-mm gun in chin turret, and two underwing hardpoints on each stub wing can accommodate weapons which include XM18E1 0.3-in (7.62-mm) Minigun pods, and XM157 (seven-tube) or X159 (19-tube) folding-fin rocket pods; (AH-1T) eight TOW missiles in four two-round launchers on outboard stub wing hardpoints, plus other weapons on vacant hardpoints and XM197 gun in chin turret

*Bell AH-1G, the original single-engine Cobra version.*

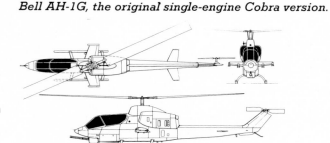

*Bell AH-1T Improved SeaCobra*

'The widespread use of the helicopter was the most significant advance of the Vietnam War. Combined with a new air-assault concept, it led to the refinement of the airmobile division that proved to be an unqualified success, incorporating all the advantages that the helicopter provided. It is difficult to exaggerate the capabilities of the airmobile team in Vietnam; the team represented the most revolutionary change in warfare since the blitzkrieg.'

The US Army's conclusion may be arguable, but its enthusiasm certainly is not. The proper use of the helicopter added a totally new dimension to the US Army's operations, freeing local commanders from many of the restrictions that terrain, the enemy, logistics and conventional tactics had imposed upon them in earlier times.

## European war zone

Today's United States Army is a small organization by contemporary standards, built around general-purpose forces and really aimed at fighting a war in Europe, in conjunction with NATO allies. It shares a simple mission with NATO forces and the combined air power of the US Air Force and US Navy. It must help to stop an enemy invasion in its tracks, and hold it until either a negotiated peace can be obtained, or until reinforcements arrive as replacements.

The US Army uses helicopters as organic equipment, assigned to accompany division fighting teams into action and to support them as they move across and hold terrain. Five types

*Though a multi-purpose transport rather than a dedicated crane helicopter, the Boeing Vertol Chinook is second to none among Western tactical helicopters in lifting ability, with a centre hook for a load of 28,000 lb (12701 kg). The US Army is having surviving CH-47As remanufactured to CH-47D standard.*

*The concept of the Tarhe is simple: attach helicopter components to a long beam so that loads can be straddled, hoisted and moved. In Vietnam, these rugged cranes retrieved almost 400 damaged aircraft during a trial evaluation. Trucks, fuel, broken aircraft, even a van full of 87 combat-ready troops have been lifted by Sikorsky CH-54s.*

of US Army units use helicopters: assault helicopter companies, attack helicopter companies, general support companies, aerial rocket artillery battalions, and air cavalry troops. These use armed helicopters in several fundamental missions: armed escort, security for observation helicopters, direct fire support against assigned targets, and as aerial rocket artillery.

One of the problems of which the US Army is aware is that offensive tactics developed for Vietnam may be nearly useless in a defensive European war. One such tactic (air assault) was used on the offensive in Vietnam, and was an innovation in the deployment of US Army manoeuvre elements. Helicopters reconnoitred the area, softened it with rocket artillery if necessary, moved in a ground control party, and followed it with the main body of troops, together with their supplies and equipment. Above all this orbited an airborne command post, with the force commander and liaison personnel. Finally, heavy-lift helicopters were brought up

*A solitary HueyCobra gunship, a late AH-1S model, hovers a few feet off the ground with weapons at the ready. Armament includes eight TOW anti-tank missiles on the outer pylons.*

# The Army's Air Strength

to move or position howitzers or other heavy equipment, and to recover any downed helicopters lost during the movement.

It is as a fighting machine that the US Army sees the helicopter best employed in a European scenario. The helicopter is very versatile and capable, and can be fitted to carry a wide range of current armament, both guns and missiles. Skilfully handled, it flies nap-of-the-earth patterns, skimming the ground, using terrain and trees for concealment. It pops out of hiding, fires a missile or a burst from a gun pack at a target of opportunity, and drops back into hiding again. So far, that type of operation is simply an extension of what was done in Vietnam and practised thousands of times since. But in the intervening years, armament technology has combined with advances in helicopter design to produce a lethal and efficient killing machine.

## Deadly games against the choppers

It is not usual to think of the helicopter as a fighter capable of air combat against fighters. But it is exactly that. The appearance of the Russian-designed Mil Mi-24 helicopter gunship in the armies of the Warsaw Pact countries, and the way it was used in Pact military exercises, galvanized both the US Army and the USAF's Tactical Air Command. In a series of joint training and educational exercises conducted a couple of years ago, helicopters simulating the Mi-24 worked in conjunction with simulated Pact radar sites and missile batteries to duplicate the Russian tactics and derive countering tactics. The agile helicopters were able to destroy (simulated, of course) the range of fighters and fighter-bombers that TAC threw into the arena. Over a ridge would slide a Vought A-7, its pilot intent on dropping a couple of Mk 82 bombs into the middle of a missile battery. And as he steadied for the run-in, a helicopter would pop out of cover, fix him for an instant in its sights, and launch a theoretical missile or fire a theoretical burst that would nail the attacker almost every time. It was a sobering experience for the fighter pilots of TAC, and an enlightening one for the US Army helicopter pilots who participated in the exercise. It began to look as if there was no way to beat the helicopters. If they saw you, you were dead. If you saw them first, you had a chance of evading them. But maybe that evasion set you up for a direct shot from an anti-aircraft artillery battery or a surface-to-air missile. It was a very deadly game.

And so it is. Helicopters are like that: they can engage in combat against the finest fighters and, if the fixed-wing pilots are a little careless, win the fight every time.

The other great advantage the helicopter offers is as airborne artillery. The US Army depends heavily on its artillery: before an advance, artillery softens enemy positions; against a tank assault, it is a primary defensive weapon; and it supports troops in the field, whether they are moving or pinned down or stationed, as they were in Vietnam, in fire-support bases designed to

*Bell's Kiowa 'chopper', shown here in the OH-58C development model, has a flat-front windscreen for better visibility.*

*Rockets ripple away from one of the high-tail prototypes of the AH-64 attack helicopter. Subsequently almost every part was redesigned, a process taking seven years and causing a severe escalation in unit price. The result is a much better helicopter, but it is highly doubtful that the US Army will be able to afford all its planned buy of 536.*

make the enemy come out and fight.

Helicopters were used extensively in Vietnam to move and position artillery. They were big, available skyhooks, and they gave an artillery unit far more mobility than it could achieve in the usual way. But then the helicopter itself became flying artillery, using a variety of weapons in that role. Designated as aerial rocket artillery (ARA), the helicopter as field gun was one of the major innovations to come out of Vietnam.

In that conflict it was organized and employed as just another artillery piece. Supporting fire was requested through the usual channels, generally from a forward observer. Helicopter artillery had a number of advantages over conventional artillery, but its most outstanding was that it was almost instantly available when the infantry badly needed it, just after they had hit the landing zone.

The standard helicopter artillery rounds were M3 2.75-in (69.85-mm) folding-fin rockets that could be triggered in single shots or ripple fire, and hit targets out to 2 miles (3.2 km) distant. Their high-explosive warheads were equivalent to those thrown by 107-mm (4.2-in) mortars. Additionally, the ARA helicopters carried wire-guided anti-tank missiles. The North Vietnamese or the Viet Cong had few tanks; but the missiles were most useful against point targets anywhere.

Most direct comparisons favouring the ARA were made against the 105-mm (4.13-in) howitzer, a standard field piece with the US Army since World War I. The late-model lightweight

*Popularly called the 'Loach', from its LOH (light observation helicopter) role, the Hughes OH-6A is the Army's smallest, fastest and most nimble rotary-wing machine. It can be adapted to carry light weapons. Despite its excellent reputation the US Army has not bought the much more sophisticated and aggressive derivative, the Hughes 500 M-D Defender equipped with TOW missiles, telescopic nose sights and highly effective 30-mm Hughes Chain Gun.*

# Sikorsky UH-60 Black Hawk

**SPECIFICATION**

**Type:** (UH-60A) combat assault squad transport; (SH-60B) ship-based multi-purpose helicopter

**Powerplant:** two 1,543-shp (1151-kW) General Electric T700-GE-700

**Performance:** (UH-60A) maximum speed 184 mph (296 km/h) at sea level; maximum speed at maximum take-off weight 182 mph (293 km/h); maximum cruising speed 169 mph (272 km/h) at 4,000 ft (1220 m); single-engine speed 149 mph (240 km/h); range at maximum take-off with 30-minute reserves 373 miles (600 km)

**Weights:** (UH-60A) empty 10,900 lb (4944 kg); mission take-off 16,450 lb (7462 kg); maximum take-off 20,250 lb (9185 kg)

**Dimensions:** main rotor diameter 53 ft 8 in (16.36 m); tail rotor diameter 11 ft 0 in (3.35 m); length (rotors turning) 64 ft 10 in (19.76 m); height 16 ft 10 in (5.13 m); main-rotor disc area 2,261 sq ft (210.05 m²)

**Armament:** (UH-60A) provision for one or two 7.62-mm (0.3-in) M 60 machine-guns firing from opened side doors; (SH-60B) two homing torpedoes

*One of the 1,000-plus UH-60A Black Hawks with the US Army.*

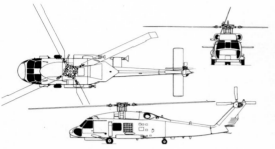

*Sikorsky SH-60B Seahawk*

*UH-60A assigned to the 101st Airborne Division.*

M102 105 weighs in at around 3,200 lb (1470 kg), has a crew of eight, and takes three or four minutes to set up and start to fire. It can fire about three rounds per minute. Contrast that with the two-man crew of a typical gunship, its almost instant availability, and a rate of fire that can empty its rocket pods in just 6 seconds, if the target warrants such a burst of lethality.

## Airborne artillery

The armament of current attack helicopters also is heavy, and of greater variety. Typically, they can carry the NATO 7.62-mm (0.3-in) machine-gun in packs, and either the 20-mm or 30-mm automatic cannon packs. Additionally, they load multiple 40-mm grenade-launchers and 2.75-in (69.85-mm) rockets. Apart from these, there may be paired pods stowing TOW missiles,

*Sikorsky's UH-60 Black Hawk series is the US Army's newest assault helicopter. Using the latest technology, the Black Hawk carries a three-man crew and 11 equipped troopers in a high-performance airframe.*

# Grumman OV-1 Mohawk

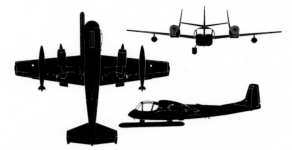

**SPECIFICATION**
**Type:** two-seat multi-sensor observation aircraft
**Powerplant:** (OV-1D) two 1,400-shp (1044-kW) Lycoming T53-L-701 turboprops
**Performance:** (OV-1D) maximum speed at maximum rated power (SLAR mission) 289 mph (465 km/h) at 10,000 ft (3050 m), (IR mission) 305 mph (491 km/h); maximum range with auxiliary fuel (SLAR mission) 944 miles (1519 km), (IR mission) 1,011 miles (1627 km); maximum endurance at 161 mph (259 km/h) at 15,000 ft (4570 m) on a SLAR mission 4 hours 20 minutes, on an IR mission 4 hours 32 minutes
**Weights:** (OV-1D) empty equipped 12,054 lb (5468 kg); normal take-off (SLAR mission) 15,741 lb (7140 kg), (IR mission) 15,544 lb (7051 kg); maximum take-off (SLAR mission) 18,109 lb (8214 kg), (IR mission) 17,912 lb (8125 kg)
**Dimensions:** span (OV-1A/-1C) 42 ft 0 in (12.80 m), (OV-1B/-1D) 48 ft 0 in (14.63 m); length 41 ft 0 in (12.50 m); height 12 ft 8 in (3.86 m); wing area

*US Army Grumman OV-1B Mohawk of the 23rd Special Warfare Aviation Detachment.*

(OV/1A/-1C) 330 sq ft (30.66 m²), (OV-1B/-1D) 360 sq ft (33.44 m²)
**Armament:** normally none, but bombs, rockets and Minigun pods have been carried on underwing pylons

*Grumman OV-1B Mohawk with SLAR*

*Only remnant of the US Army's fixed-wing air strength, this Grumman Mohawk slices in on a target, loosing four of its unguided 2.75-in (69.85-mm) rockets.*

for knocking out single tanks. The helicopter in US Army use has come a long way from the 'casevac choppers' of Korea. As the preponderant member of the US Army's air team, it has captured most of the publicity. But the US Army still operates a fixed-wing aircraft, the Grumman OV-1 Mohawk, used for battlefield surveillance, armed reconnaissance, and electronic warfare and reconnaissance. While not the close-support aircraft it was once intended to become, the Mohawk has soldiered on faithfully and is performing its special missions in a way that complements the US Army's air component of helicopters.

If it should come to war anywhere, US Army helicopter pilots are going to be aerial point men of the fighting teams. In their many skills, and in the capabilities of their helicopters, the US Army has a versatile and lethal weapon system: a combined airborne artillery piece, a close support aircraft, and an air combat fighter.

# Naval and Marine Air Power

Though it deploys powerful forces of land-based aircraft, the core of the US Navy's air power is 14 Air Wings, each based on a giant carrier. Their aircraft are among the toughest and most highly developed in history. The US Marines deploy tactical air power in support of surface assault forces.

*The wings are all the way back, and this Tomcat is ready for an air defence mission, with four AIM-54A Phoenix missiles under its fuselage for long-range engagement of targets, and a pair each of AIM-7 Sparrow and AIM-9 Sidewinders.*

*The light path traces the flight path of a catapulted Tomcat, flung off the forward carrier deck at night.*

The aircraft-carrier is the capital ship of the United States Navy. Battle groups built around it are the forward projection of America's sea power, and a symbol of the country's political and military policies.

The US Navy currently operates a combat air arm dominated by attack aircraft. There are about 1,100 of them in the inventory, as against 700 fighters, and less than 700 patrol, anti-submarine, and airborne early warning types. These do not represent the force available to the carriers, however; these figures reflect the total inventories of different types.

The US Navy's carrier-based aircraft are organized into a dozen multi-purpose air wings (MPAW), one to each of the operational large-deck carriers. Each MPAW typically includes: two fighter squadrons, each with 12 aircraft, either Grumman F-14A Tomcats or McDonnell Douglas F-4J Phantom IIs; two light attack squadrons, equipped with 12 Vought A-7E Corsair II aircraft each; one medium attack squadron with 10 Grumman A-6E Intruders; one anti-

# Gruman F-14 Tomcat

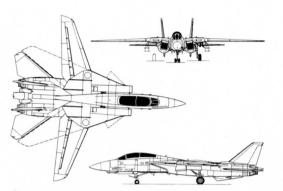

*F-14A Tomcat of Fighting Squadron 32 aboard the USS* John F. Kennedy

## SPECIFICATION

**Type:** tandem two-seat carrier-borne multi-role fighter

**Powerplant:** two 20,900-lb (9480-kg) static thrust Pratt & Whitney TF30-P-412A afterburning turbofans

**Performance:** maximum speed at altitude Mach 2.34 or 1,564 mph (2517 km/h); maximum speed at sea level Mach 1.2 or 910 mph (1470 km/h); range (interceptor, with external fuel) about 2,000 miles (3200 km); service ceiling over 56,000 ft (17070 m); maximum rate of climb at sea level (normal gross weight) over 30,000 ft (9145 m) per minute

**Weights:** empty 39,310 lb (17830 kg); normal take-off 58,539 lb (26553 kg); take-off with four Sparrows 58,904 lb (26718 kg); take-off with six Phoenix 69,790 lb (31656 kg); maximum take-off 74,348 lb (33724 kg)

**Dimensions:** span unswept 64 ft 1½ in (19.45 m); span swept 38 ft 2½ in (11.65 m); length 61 ft 2 in (18.89 m); height 16 ft 0 in (4.88 m); wing area 565.0 sq ft (52.49 m²)

**Armament:** one General Electric M61A-1 20-mm multi-barrel Vulcan cannon in forward fuselage with 675 rounds; four AIM-7 Sparrow or AIM-54 Phoenix air-to-air missiles under fuselage; two AIM-9 Sidewinder air-to-air missiles under fuselage; two AIM-9 Sidewinder air-to-air missiles, or one Sidewinder plus one Phoenix or Sparrow, under each wing glove box; tactical reconnaissance pod containing cameras and electro-optical sensors; or up to 14,500 lb (6577 kg) of Mk 82/83/84 bombs or other weapons

*Gruman F-14A Tomcat*

submarine squadron with 10 Lockheed S-3A Vikings; one squadron of eight Sikorsky SH-3A Sea King helicopters for logistics support, and for search and rescue; one squadron of Gruman EA-6B Prowlers to handle the electronic warfare mission; and one all-weather reconnaissance squadron, flying RF-4s.

Additionally, the US Navy operates 24 shore-based patrol squadrons, equipped with Lockheed P-3C Orions, a dozen per squadron. US Navy Reserve air forces include two more fighter wings and seven attack wings, plus a number of the other kinds of units that make up naval air power.

The carrier and its complement of 90 or even more aircraft is a powerful weapon. But it is also a very tempting target: sink one carrier, and knock out nearly 10 per cent of the US Navy's air power at one blow. So air defence of individual carriers and the battle group they steam with is

*Smack on the glide slope, right over the centreline, this returning Gruman F-14A Tomcat of Fighting Squadron 32 gets the cut to slam down on the deck of the USS* John F. Kennedy *(CV-67).*

*Cruising serenely above solid cloud cover, this KA-6D Intruder tanker can offload as much as 21,000 lb (9526 kg) of fuel to receiving aircraft through the probe-and-drogue system partially submerged in its belly.*

a major concern, and one the US Navy rehearses in realistic simulations and manoeuvres.

The current air defence of a battle group places a pair of airborne Grumman E-2C Hawkeye early-warning aircraft about 200 miles (320 km) ahead and well abeam of the group, covering the great dome of sky above and around the fleet elements. Each of these planes is working with a pair of Grumman Tomcats on combat air patrol. They are the advance guard: first to find, first to fight. The Tomcats carry a mix of ordnance, from long-range Phoenix missiles, with their beyond-visual-range capability, to the close-in dog-(or cat-)fighting cannon. As the spearpoint of the defence, these fighters and AEW aircraft monitor and patrol the outer zone of a three-zone system.

## Prowling amongst enemy electronics

Between them and the battle group is a middle zone, where fighters and ship-launched anti-aircraft missiles will defend the carrier and its screening force. In that zone, also, lurk the electronic warfare EA-6B Prowlers, to confuse, decoy, and out-shout enemy electronics.

Finally, a ring of fire thrown up by the ships themselves constitutes the inner zone of defence. Their batteries of anti-aircraft missiles and rapid-firing radar-directed automatic cannon are the close defence of the battle group.

Actual or simulated battle is, of course, not nearly as simple as these three clearly defined zones of defence might hint. The whole panoply of offensive and defensive tactics is brought

*The Tophatters of VF-14, one of the senior fighting squadrons in the US Navy, operated this Grumman F-14A Tomcat as part of Carrier Air Wing 1 on board the USS John F. Kennedy.*

*The unusual camouflage pattern on this Grumman F-14A Tomcat planned to create deception during manoeuvres, by confusing enemy fighter pilots about the direction and magnitude of turns.*

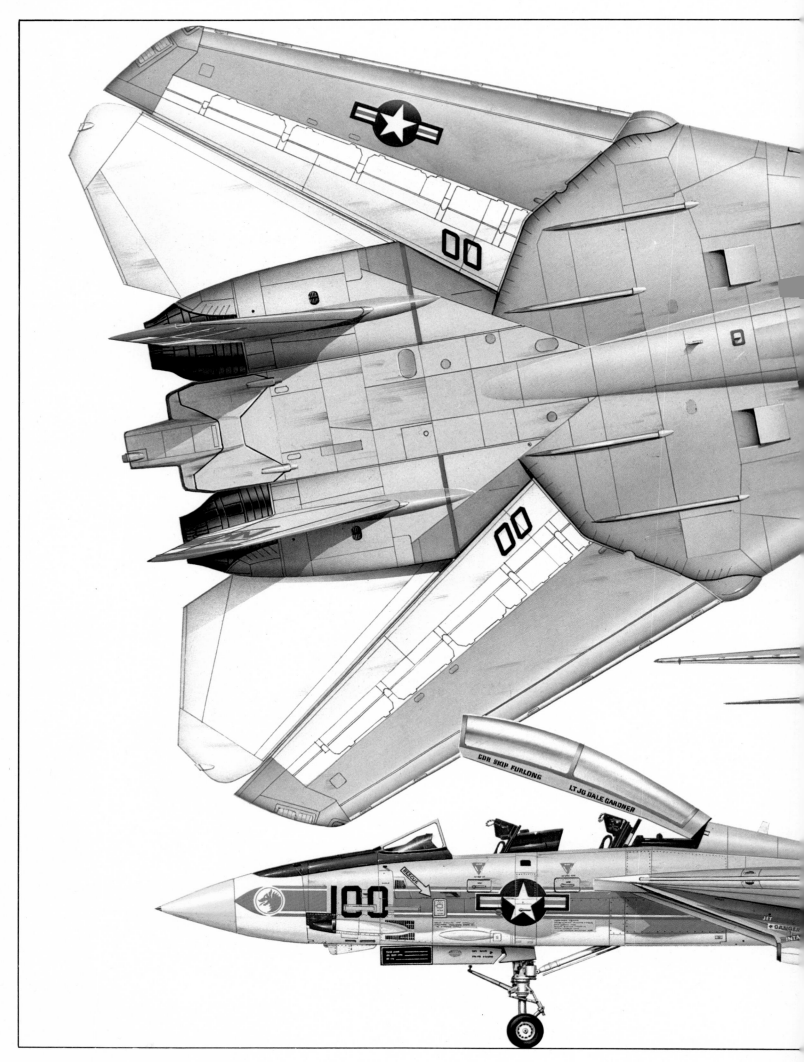

# Grumman F-14A Tomcat

*Fighting Squadron I, the famed 'Wolf Pack', emblazoned their mark prominently on the vertical tail of this F-14A Tomcat. With twin engines, a maze of electronics, a two-man crew, thin wings with big flaps and slats, and a massive pivot mechanism, is there any room for fuel? Yet the Tomcat can go to fight more than 400 miles (644 km) from its home carrier.*

## Grumman F-14A Tomcat cutaway drawing key

1 Pitot tube
2 Radar target horn
3 Glassfibre radome
4 IFF aerial array
5 Hughes AWG-9 flat plate scanner
6 Scanner tracking mechanism
7 Ventral ALQ-100 antenna
8 Gun muzzle blast trough
9 Radar electronics equipment bay
10 AN/ASN-92 inertial navigation unit
11 Radome hinge
12 In-flight refuelling probe (extended)
13 ADF aerial
14 Windscreen rain removal air duct
15 Temperature probe
16 Cockpit front pressure bulkhead
17 Angle of attack transmitter
18 Formation lighting strip
19 Cannon barrels
20 Nosewheel doors
21 Gun gas vents
22 Rudder pedals
23 Cockpit pressurisation valve
24 Navigation radar display
25 Control column
26 Instrument panel shroud
27 Kaiser AN/ANG-12 head-up display
28 Windscreen panels
29 Cockpit canopy cover
30 Face blind seat firing handle
31 Ejection seat headrest
32 Pilot's Martin-Baker GRU-7A ejection seat
33 Starboard side console panel
34 Engine throttle levers
35 Port side console panel
36 Pitot static head
37 Canopy emergency release handle
38 Fold out step
39 M-61-A1 Vulcan 20-mm six-barrel rotary cannon
40 Nose undercarriage leg strut
41 Catapult strop link
42 Catapult strop, launch position
43 Twin nosewheels
44 Folding boarding ladder
45 Hughes AIM-54A Phoenix air-to-air missile (6)
46 Fuselage missile pallet
47 Cannon ammunition drum (675 rounds)
48 Rear boarding step
49 Ammunition feed chute
50 Armament control panels
51 Kick-in step
52 Tactical information display hand controller
53 Naval Flight Officer's instrument console
54 NFO's ejection seat
55 Starboard intake lip
56 Ejection seat launch rails
57 Cockpit aft decking
58 Electrical system controller
59 Rear radio and electronics equipment bay
60 Boundary layer bleed air duct

61 Port engine intake lip
62 Electrical system relay controls
63 Glove vane pivot
64 Port air intake
65 Glove vane housing
66 Navigation light
67 Variable area intake ramp doors
68 Cooling system boundary layer duct ram air intake
69 Intake ramp door hydraulic jacks
70 Air system piping
71 Air data computer
72 Heat exchanger
73 Heat exchanger exhaust duct
74 Forward fuselage fuel tanks
75 Canopy hinge point
76 Electrical and control system ducting
77 Control rod runs
78 UHF/TACAN aerial
79 Glove vane hydraulic jack
80 Starboard glove vane, extended
81 Honeycomb panel construction
82 Navigation light
83 Main undercarriage wheel bay
84 Starboard intake duct spill door
85 Wing slat/flap flexible drive shaft
86 Dorsal spine fairing
87 Fuselage top longeron
88 Central flap/slat drive
89 Emergency hydraulic generator
90 Bypass door hydraulic jack
91 Intake bypass door
92 Port intake ducting
93 Wing glove sealing horn
94 Flap/slat telescopic drive shaft
95 Port wing pivot bearing
96 Wing pivot carry through (electron beam welded)
97 Wing pivot box integral fuel tank
98 Fuselage longeron/pivot box attachment joint
99 UHF data link/IFF aerial
100 Honeycomb skin panelling
101 Wing glove stiffeners/dorsal fences
102 Starboard wing pivot bearing
103 Slat/flap drive shaft gearbox
104 Starboard wing integral fuel tank (total internal fuel capacity 2364 US gal/8951 litres)
105 Leading edge slat drive shaft
106 Slat guide rails
107 Starboard leading edge slat segments (open)
108 Starboard navigation light

109 Low-voltage formation lighting
110 Wing tip fairing
111 Outboard manoeuvre flap segments (down position)
112 Port roll control spoilers
113 Spoiler hydraulic jacks
114 Inboard, high lift flap (down position)
115 Inboard flap hydraulic jack
116 Manoeuvre flap drive shaft
117 Variable wing sweep jack
118 Starboard main undercarriage pivot fixing
119 Starboard engine compressor face
120 Wing glove sealing plates
121 Pratt & Whitney TF30-P-412 afterburning turbofan
122 Rear fuselage fuel tanks
123 Fuselage longeron joint
124 Control system artificial feel units
125 Tailplane control rods
126 Starboard engine bay
127 Wing glove pneumatic seal
128 Fin root fairing
129 Fin spar attachment joints
130 Starboard fin leading edge
131 Starboard all-moving tailplane
132 Starboard wing (fully swept position)
133 AN/ALR-45 tail warning radar antenna
134 Fin aluminium honeycomb skin panel construction
135 Fin-tip aerial fairing
136 Tail navigation light
137 Electronic counter-measures antenna (ECM)
138 Rudder honeycomb construction
139 Rudder hydraulic jack
140 Afterburner ducting
141 Variable area nozzle control jack
142 Airbrake (upper and lower surfaces)
143 Airbrake hydraulic jack
144 Starboard engine exhaust nozzle
145 Anti-collision light
146 Tail formation light
147 ECM aerial
148 Port rudder
149 Beaver tail fairing
150 Fuel jettison pipe

151 ECM antenna
152 Deck arrester hook (stowed position)
153 AN/ALE-29A chaff and flare dispensers
154 Nozzle shroud sealing flaps
155 Port convergent/divergent afterburner exhaust nozzle
156 Tailplane honeycomb construction
157 AN/ALR-45(V) tail warning radar antenna
158 Tailplane boron fibre skin panels
159 Port wing (fully swept position)
160 All-moving-tailplane construction
161 Tailplane pivot fixing
162 Jet pipe mounting
163 Fin/tailplane attachment mainframe
164 Cooling air louvres
165 Tailplane hydraulic jack
166 Hydraulic system equipment pack
167 Formation lighting strip
168 Oil cooler air intake
169 Port vental fin
170 Engine accessory compartment
171 Ventral engine access doors
172 Hydraulic reservoir
173 Bleed air ducting
174 Port engine bay
175 Intake compressor face
176 Wing variable sweep screw jack
177 Main undercarriage leg strut
178 Hydraulic retraction jack
179 Wing skin panel
180 Fuel system piping
181 Rear spar
182 Flap hinge brackets
183 Port roll control spoilers
184 Flap leading edge eyebrow seal fairing
185 Port manoeuvre flap honeycomb construction
186 Wing tip fairing construction

187 Low-voltage formation lighting
188 Port navigation light
189 Wing rib construction
190 Port wing integral fuel tank
191 Front spar
192 Leading edge rib construction
193 Slat guide rails
194 Port leading edge slat segments, open
195 Slat honeycomb construction

196 Port mainwheel
197 Torque scissor links
198 Main undercarriage front bracing strut
199 Mainwheel well door
200 Ventral pylon attachment
201 External fuel tank (capacity 265 US gal/1011 litres)
202 Sparrow missile launch adaptor
203 AIM-7F Sparrow air-to-air missile

204 Wing glove pylon attachment
205 Cranked wing glove pylon
206 Sidewinder missile launch rail
207 AIM-9C Sidewinder air-to-air missile
208 Phoenix launch pallet
209 AIM-54A Phoenix air-to-air missile

*F-14A of VF-143 ('The Pukin' Dogs'), CVW-6 aboard USS America (CV-66).*

AVIAGRAPHICA

# Grumman Hawkeye

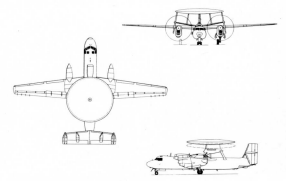

*Grumman E-2C operated from the USS* Constellation *by VAW-126.*

*Grumman E-2C Hawkeye*

*Grumman E-2 Hawkeye.*

**SPECIFICATION**
**Type:** airborne early-warning and control aircraft
**Powerplant:** two 4,910-shp (3661-kW) Allison T56-A-425 turboprops
**Performance:** maximum speed 374 mph (602 km/h); cruising speed for maximum range 310 mph (499 km/h); patrol endurance 6 hours; maximum ferry range 1,605 miles (2583 km); service ceiling 30,800 ft (9390 m)
**Weights:** empty 37,678 lb (17090 kg); internal fuel load 12,400 lb (5624 kg); maximum take-off 51,569 lb (23391 kg)
**Dimensions:** span 80 ft 7 in (24.56 m); length 57 ft 7 in (17.55 m); height 18 ft 4 in (5.59 m); wing area 700.0 sq ft (65.03 m²)
**Armament:** none

into play, and action will cross the boundaries from one zone to the next. But this is the basic arrangement, and every indication is that it is an effective one. It would be the defence of choice against, for example, a Russian strike at the 6th Fleet in the Persian Gulf, with a regiment or two of supersonic Tupolev Tu-22M (Tu-26) 'Backfire' maritime strike bombers slashing in from a forward base in Afghanistan.

Another serious threat of long standing is the submarine, able to dive deep and to cruise rapidly while submerged, taking advantage of water temperatures, coastal echoes, and a variety of the submariner's tricks to avoid detection. As one modern move in the defence against submarine attack, the US Navy developed the LAMPS (Light Airborne Multi-Purpose System) team of helicopter and surface vessel. Its mission is two-fold: anti-submarine warfare, and anti-ship surveillance and targeting. Both helicopter and ship carry sensors and weapons:

*A US Navy Vought A-7E carrying the tailcode of Carrier Air Wing 2 landing on CVA-61, the USS* Ranger, *a 'Forrestal'- class carrier assigned to the Pacific Fleet.*

*One of the USS* John F. Kennedy's *Hawkeyes picks up the first wire, beside a parked S-3A. COD (Carrier On-board Delivery) is performed by the C-2A Greyhound version.*

# Naval and Marine Air Power

*The Sikorsky SH-3D anti-submarine helicopter equipped about 10 squadrons at the height of its service.*

*Kaman's SH-2F is standard interim LAMPS helicopter deployed in eight squadrons aboard surface warships, including the FF-1052 ('Knox'-class) frigates of the type seen astern. The sensors include LN-66HP radar under the nose and the MAD (magnetic-anomaly detector) 'bird' seen prominently slung under the outboard pylon.*

*The immense volume of the nose radome of the two-seat attack A-6 is evident in this A-6E drawn to the same scale as the Prowler below. Unit is VA-65 ('Tigers') of CVW-7 aboard USS Independence.*

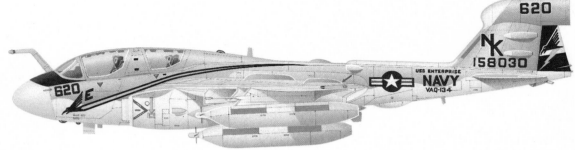

*The Intruder became a Prowler by lengthening the nose and adding a tail pod. Those are the external, obvious changes; but under the skin, this EA-6B is crammed with electronic countermeasures galore. There are more than 30 different antennae as part of the ECM installation, and their intake and output keep the four-man crew busy.*

*The US Navy's carrier-based ASW platform is the S-3A Viking, an amazing package of complex systems plus four humans. About 160 are expected to be retrofitted with improved sensors and the Harpoon missile to become S-3Bs.*

Harpoon anti-ship missiles on the ship, and a pair of Mk 46 homing torpedoes on the helicopter. Currently, LAMPS Mk I is built around the Kaman SH-2F Seasprite helicopter; by early 1984, the Sikorsky SH-60B Seahawk will be phasing in as part of the LAMPS Mk III programme.

Basically, LAMPS extends the sensing range of US Navy ships (cruisers, destroyers or frigates) beyond their visual and electronic horizons. Without the added capability of the airborne sensors, those fighting ships were limited by sensor technology to about a 20-mile (32-km) radius in a search for submarines. But the addition of helicopter-borne sensors increases that number several times over, and multiplies the area of ocean under the influence of a single ship by a factor of 20 or more. The armed helicopter is more than a sensor platform, because it can launch its homing torpedoes either on command from the mother ship or on the initiative of the helicopter crew, if they are so authorized.

# BAe/McDonnell Douglas AV-8A/AV-8B

**SPECIFICATION**
**McDonnell Douglas AV-8B**
**Advanced Harrier**
**Type:** V/STOL strike aircraft
**Powerplant:** one 21,500-lb (9752-kg) thrust Rolls-Royce Pegasus Mk 803 (F402-RR-402) vectored-thrust turbofan
**Performance:** (estimated) operational radius (VTO) with 3,000-lb (1361-kg) external load 57 miles (92 km); operational radius (STO) with same external load 414 miles (666 km); ferry range over 2,000 miles (3220 km)
**Weights:** basic operating empty 12,470 lb (5656 kg); maximum take-off (VTO) 18,850 lb (8550 kg); maximum take-off (STO) 29,750 lb (13495 kg)
**Dimensions:** span 30 ft 4 in (9.25 m); length 46 ft 4 in (14.12 m); height 11 ft 7¾ in (3.55 m); wing area 230 sq ft (21.37 m²)
**Armament:** twin underfuselage gun/ammunition packs each mounting a US 20-mm cannon or 30-mm Aden gun; three underfuselage and six underwing hardpoints with combined capacity of 9,200 lb (4173 kg); weapons carried can include Mk 82 Snakeye bombs and laser or electro-optical guided weapons, and AIM-9L Sidewinders for air-to-air use

*AV-8A Harrier of Marine Corps squadron VMA-231.*

*BAe/McDonnell Douglas AV-8B*

*BAe/McDonnell Douglas AV-8A.*

US Marine Corps aviation is unique. It has evolved over the years from a single uncompromising principle, stated by Alfred A. Cunningham, the first USMC aviator, after reviewing the experiences of the US Marine Corps in World War I: 'The only excuse for aviation in any service is its usefulness in assisting troops on the ground to successfully carry out their operations.'

At the core of US Marine aviation is the US Marine mission of amphibious operations. The combat air arm is geared to the requirements of a landing force. It must be flexible and responsive to immediate needs; it must support and work closely with the ground elements. As a result of years of experience, today's US Marine Corps aviation is a co-equal member of the air-ground team.

## Amphibious operations

The basic principles of air-ground co-operation were developed early in the history of US Marine aviation. When US Marines were sent to Nicaragua in 1927 to support government forces trying to put down an insurrection, it became very apparent that air elements could play a vital role in the fighting. How best to work that problem, and how to co-ordinate the two disparate force elements of foot-soldier and airman, occupied the planners during that campaign. World War II was the first opportunity to try out, on a large scale, the doctrines and tactics that had been evolving with the US Marine Corps. In that war, US Marine fighter-bombers spearheaded the island-hopping invasions that rolled back the Japanese. In later engagements in Korea, US Marine aviators, their skills honed after four years of invasion support in the Pacific, turned in outstanding performances in support of ground troops.

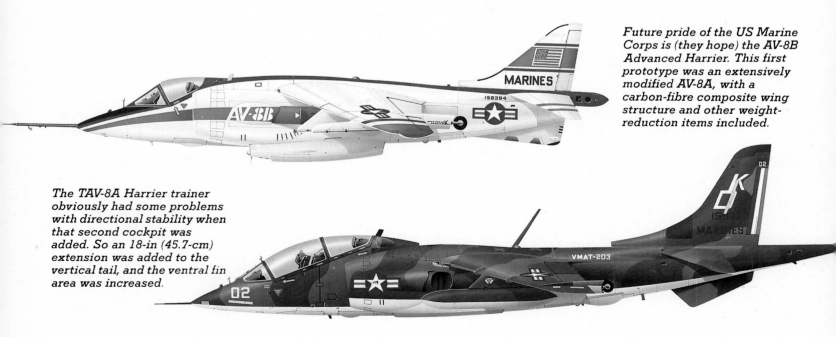

*Future pride of the US Marine Corps is (they hope) the AV-8B Advanced Harrier. This first prototype was an extensively modified AV-8A, with a carbon-fibre composite wing structure and other weight-reduction items included.*

*The TAV-8A Harrier trainer obviously had some problems with directional stability when that second cockpit was added. So an 18-in (45.7-cm) extension was added to the vertical tail, and the ventral fin area was increased.*

*Photographic Phantom is this US Marine RF-4B from VMCJ-2. It's a rare bird; only 46 were built, out of the total of more than 5,000 Phantoms of all types produced.*

*In theory these are low-contrast markings, and they probably reduce the glint substantially. But the photographers from VMFP-3, a photo-reconnaissance squadron based at El Toro, California, should recognise contrast when they see it, and this bird has it.*

Another aspect of Marine aviation uniqueness is its organization as an expeditionary air arm. Since US Marine Corps doctrines call for air support of ground forces from before the landings through all subsequent operations, it was apparent that US Marine aviators would have to operate from carriers and land bases alike, and that the latter could be expected to be primitive facilities.

## Fixed and rotary

US Marine aviation is organized in three Marine Air Wings (MAW), one assigned to each of the three US Marine divisions specified by law. A fourth air-ground team is organized as a Marine Reserve division. Like other air arms, US Marine aviation uses both fixed- and rotary-wing aircraft. The fixed-wing aircraft are fighters, like the McDonnell Douglas F-4 Phantom II, standard mount of the US Marine tactical fighter squadrons, and attackers, a mix of McDonnell Douglas A-4 Skyhawks, Grumman A-6 Intruders, and three squadrons of British Aerospace AV-8A Harriers. They total 25 squadrons. For observation, reconnaissance and forward air control, the US Marines have a number of Rockwell International OV-10A Broncos.

The helicopter force is split into four types of squadrons, each built around a single model of helicopter. Heavy assault support squadrons fly the Sikorsky CH-53 Sea Stallion models;

*Paired US Marine Corps Phantoms (F-4N models) take on fuel from the probe-and-drogue system of a US Marine KC-130F tanker/transport.*

# McDonnell Douglas F-18

*The first US Navy Hornet squadron was VFA-125 based at NAS Lemoore, California. In early 1982 they put up a tremendous show in a squadron deployment to the Nevada desert, firing 28,000 rounds and dropping 1,600 bombs with consistently better accuracy than the A-7E that the F/A-18 will eventually replace. This bird is carrying two AIM-9L Sidewinders on the wingtips and two Sparrow medium-range AAMs on the body pylons.*

*First flown on 18 November 1978, the F/A-18 Hornet is a true multi-role aircraft able to replace both interceptors and all-weather attack aircraft. The Department of Defense intends to buy 1,366 Hornets for the US Navy and Marine Corps. The first Navy squadron became operational in 1982.*

## McDonnell Douglas F-18 Hornet cutaway drawing key

1 Radome
2 Radar scanner (see item 9)
3 Scanner drive mechanism
4 Gun muzzle
5 Gun gas vents
6 Cannon barrels
7 Radar package sliding rails
8 Low voltage formation lighting
9 Hughes AN/APG-65 multi-mode radar package
10 Infra-red sensor housing
11 Ammunition drum, 540 rounds
12 Angle of attack probe
13 Gun mounting
14 Flight refuelling probe, extended
15 Refuelling probe hydraulic jack
16 M61, 20-mm rotary cannon
17 Ammunition feed track
18 Communications antenna
19 Cockpit front bulkhead
20 Pressurization valve
21 Frameless windshield panel
22 Instrument panel shroud
23 Pilot's sight and Kaiser head-up display
24 Control column
25 Rudder pedals
26 Wing leading edge extension (LEX)

27 Nosewheel bay
28 Nosewheel doors
29 Retractable step
30 Catapult strop link, landing position
31 Strop link, launch position
32 Twin nosewheels
33 Catapult launch signal lights
34 Landing lamp
35 Cleveland nose undercarriage leg
36 Avionics bay
37 Control runs
38 Engine throttle controls
39 Pilot's port side console
40 Cockpit rear bulkhead
41 Martin-Baker SJU-5/A ejection seat
42 Starboard side console
43 Ejection seat firing handle
44 Cockpit canopy
45 Canopy open position
46 Canopy jack
47 2nd seat structural space provision (TF-18)
48 Forward fuselage fuel tank
49 Honeycomb panel construction
50 Liquid oxygen container

51 Nose undercarriage retraction strut
52 Centreline drop tank capacity 300 US gal (1136 litres)
53 Avionics bays
54 LEX frame construction
55 Port navigation light
56 Air conditioning ducting
57 Intake splitter plate
58 Air conditioning intake
59 Bleed air holes
60 Boundary layer control slot
61 Main fuel tanks, 10,860-lb (4930-kg) internal fuel load
62 Communications aerial
63 Bleed air outlet louvres

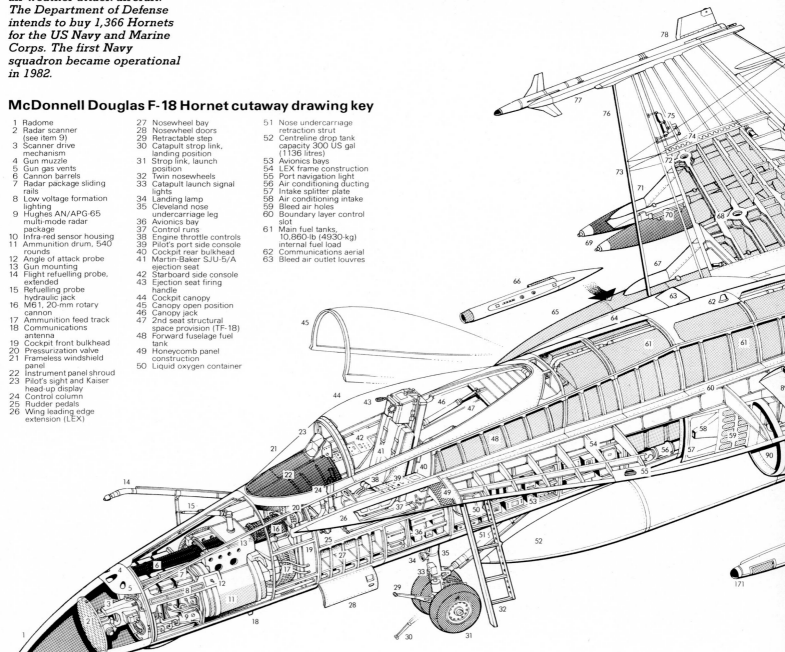

64 Starboard leading edge extension
65 External fuel tank, capacity 610 US gal (2309 litres)
66 Laser spot tracker pod (LST), starboard fuselage station
67 Starboard inboard wing pylon
68 Pylon mounting
69 Mk 83 low drag general purpose (LDGP) bombs (A-18)
70 Bomb ejector rack
71 Starboard outer wing pylon
72 Pylon fixing
73 Leading edge dog-tooth
74 Wing fold hinge line
75 Outboard leading edge acutator
76 Drooping leading edge
77 Starboard wing tip missile launcher rail
78 AIM-9L Sidewinder air-to-air missile
79 Outer wing panel folded position
80 Starboard drooping aileron
81 Starboard double slotted flap
82 Flap guides
83 Wing integral fuel tank
84 Hydraulic flap jacks
85 Graphite/epoxy dorsal fairing panels
86 Fuel delivery piping
87 Fuselage longeron
88 Boundary layer bleed air duct
89 Air conditioning plant
90 Port intake
91 Intake ducting
92 Leading edge flap hydraulic jack
93 Flap sequencing control unit
94 Control cable runs
95 Wing attachment pin joints
96 Rear fuselage fuel tank
97 APU exhaust duct
98 Starboard engine bay
99 Fin attachment fixing
100 Fin construction
101 Fuel jettison pipe
102 Graphite/epoxy skin
103 Anti-collision light
104 Steel leading edge strip
105 Honeycomb panel
106 Aerial tuners
107 Electronic counter-measures aerials (ECM)
108 Fin tip antenna housing
109 Communications aerial
110 Radar warning receiver
111 Tail navigation light
112 Fuel jettison
113 Low voltage formation lighting
114 Honeycomb rudder construction
115 Rudder hydraulic jacks
116 Airbrake open position
117 Starboard tailplane
118 Port fin tip antenna housing
119 Low voltage formation lighting
120 Airbrake housing
121 Airbrake hydraulic jack
122 Starboard engine tailpipe
123 Exhaust nozzle shroud
124 Variable area exhaust nozzle
125 Nozzle actuators
126 Afterburner duct
127 Port tailplane
128 Graphite/epoxy skin panels
129 Honeycomb construction
130 Steel leading edge strip
131 Deck arresting hook
132 Tailplane pivot
133 Tailplane hinge lever
134 Hydraulic servo actuator
135 Port engine bay
136 Engine access doors
137 Engine accessories
138 Main engine mounting
139 General Electric F404-GE-400 low bypass turbofan
140 Engine compressor face
141 Airborne auxiliary power plant (APU)
142 Airframe mounted auxiliary drive gearbox
143 Port flap actuators
144 Flap sequencing control
145 Flap guides
146 Port double slotted flap
147 Graphite/epoxy flap skins
148 Honeycomb panel construction
149 Wing fold actuator
150 Aileron hydraulic jacks
151 Fixed portion of trailing edge
152 Port wing tip AIM-9 Sidewinder
153 Missile launcher rail
154 Honeycomb leading edge construction
155 Outboard leading edge actuators
156 Outboard leading edge actuators
157 Outboard wing panel construction
158 Wing fold hinge line
159 Port outboard pylon fixing
160 Port outboard pylon
161 Bomb ejector rack
162 Mk 83 LDGP bombs
163 Leading-edge dog tooth
164 Multi-spar wing panel construction
165 Port wing integral fuel tank
166 Inboard pylon fixing
167 Cleveland main undercarriage leg
168 Pivoted axle beam
169 Port mainwheel
170 AIM-7F Sparrow air-to-air missile
171 Forward looking infra-red pod (FLIR), port fuselage station

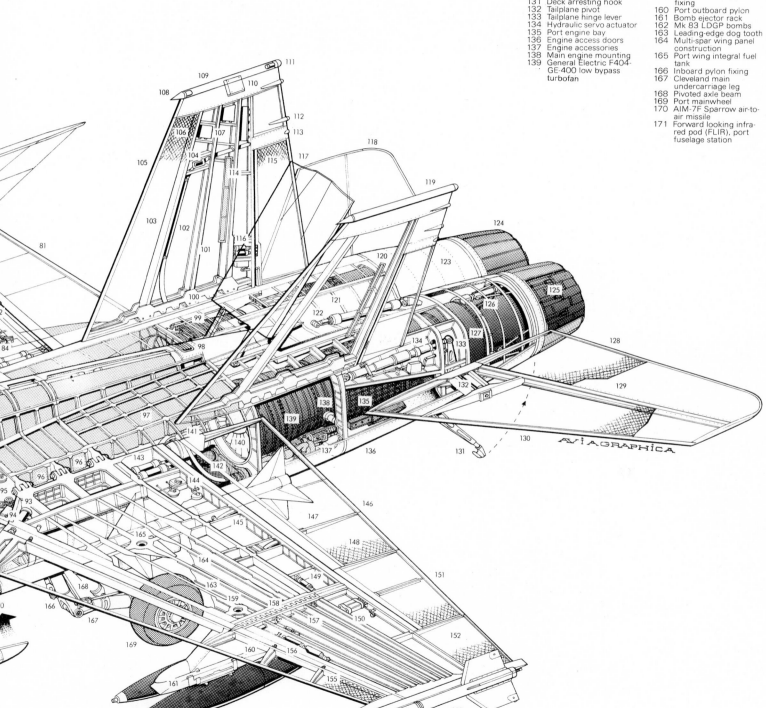

AVIAGRAPHICA

33

# McDonnell Douglas A-4 Skyhawk

### SPECIFICATION
**McDonnell Douglas A-4M Skyhawk II**
**Type:** single-seat attack bomber
**Powerplant:** one 11,200-lb (5080-kg) Pratt & Whitney J52-P-408 turbojet
**Performance:** maximum speed with 4,000-lb (1814-kg) bombload, 646 mph (1040 km/h); maximum ferry range 2,000 miles (3219 km)
**Weights:** empty 10,800 lb (4899 kg), take-off 24,500 lb (11113 kg)
**Dimensions:** 27 ft 6 in (8.38 m); length 40 ft 4 in (12.29 m); height 15 ft 0 in (4.57 m); wing area 260 sq ft (24.15 m²)
**Armament:** underfuselage hardpoint with a capacity fo 3,500 lb (1588 kg); two inboard underwing hardpoints each with a capacity of 2,250 lb (1021 kg); two outboard underwing hardpoints each with a capacity of 1,000 lb (454 kg). Extensive range of weapons can be carried, including conventional or nuclear bombs, air-to-air and air-to-ground rockets, missiles and gunpods

*A-4M Skyhawk II of Marine Squadron VMA-324.*

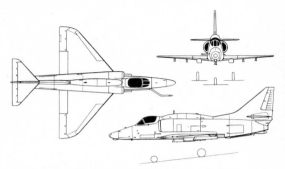

*McDonnell Douglas A-4M Skyhawk II*

*McDonnell Douglas A-4M Skyhawk II.*

medium assault support squadrons are equipped with the Boeing Vertol CH-46 Sea Knight, and light assault support squadrons fly the Bell UH-1. Additionally, the US Marines fly Bell AH-1 attack helicopters in a re-engined version called the SeaCobra. There are 26 helicopter squadrons.

## Assault tactics

US Marine operational manuals define the kinds of missions these units fly. They centre on the amphibious assault and describe, in some detail, just how the pre-invasion missions will be flown, how the landing itself will be supported, and how the aerial bombardment and strafing will move inland ahead of the US Marine riflemen. All well and good; but recent events have

*Latest, but not necessarily last, of the profusion of Skyhawk variants, the OA-4M is a rebuild of the TA-4F for US Marine Corps FAC duties. Avionics basically resemble those of the A-4M.*

*First of the Bell AH-1T Improved SeaCobras delivered to the US Marines carried high-visibility markings on rotor and tail. The first craft was a rebuild of a standard AH-1J, using new dynamic components and a twin-turbine installation.*

*The tandem-seat A-4 models have proved particularly valuable, and will certainly go on into the 1990s in US Marine Corps service. This TA-4J rocket training sortie was flown at Yuma, Arizona, by VMAT-102.*

introduced an ominous note into these orchestrations of tactics.

The Yom Kippur War in October 1973 was the turning point in thinking about air support. US Marine aviation has been able to turn the tide in its favour by bringing more aircraft into the battle to ensure control of the skies above the landing force. But now, enemy surface-to-air (SAM) missiles can maintain air superiority above their own forces. Further, those SAMs and accompanying automatic anti-aircraft artillery are mobile; they can move with the defending forces, instead of being tied to fixed bases. And that is bad news for US Marine Corps aviators. Says Marine Corps Manual FMFM 5-1: 'Offensive air support and assault support operations can no longer dominate landing force thinking. Without the capability to conduct successful electronic warfare and offensive anti-air warfare operations, the amphibious assault by any size Marine air-ground task force becomes untenable.'

*Above: The prototype YCH-53E Super Stallion is a tri-motored, seven-bladed helicopter that resembles a gross error along the production line. Its canted tail and lumpy powerplants and pods belie its truly remarkable performance. The US Marines operate production CH-53Es as heavy-lift helicopters.*

*Left: One of the more underrated combat aircraft, the OV-10A Bronco can carry a wide range of sensor systems and armament. Here the closer of the two flying over the US Army's Tropic Test Center is hauling three CBU-55 fuel-air explosive bombs, weapons of area destruction.*

*One of the first batch of 114 North American Rockwell OV-10A aircraft built for the US Marines, this example carries the current low-visibility markings and is camouflaged with a special paint to maintain a low infra-red signature.*

# Sikorsky CH-53 Sea Stallion

## SPECIFICATION

**Type:** heavy assault transport helicopter
**Powerplant:** (CH-53D) two 3,925-shp (2927-kW) General Electric T64-GE-413 turboshafts
**Performance:** (CH-53D) maximum speed at sea level 196 mph (315 km/h); cruising speed 173 mph (278 km/h); range with 4,076-lb (1849-kg) fuel, 2 minutes warm-up, cruising speed, 10% reserves 257 miles (414 km)
**Weights:** (CH-53D) empty 23,485 lb (10653 kg); mission take-off 36,400 lb (16511 kg); maximum take-off 42,000 lb (19051 kg)
**Dimensions:** main rotor diameter 72 ft 3 in (22.02 m); tail rotor diameter 16 ft 0 in (4.88 m); length (rotors turning) 88 ft 3 in (26.90 m); height 24 ft 11 in (7.59 m); main rotor disc area 4,070 sq ft (378.10 m²)

*CH-53D Sea Stallion of US Marine Heavy Helicopter Squadron 462 (HMH-462) based at Okinawa.*

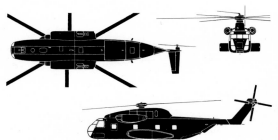

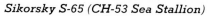

*Sikorsky S-65 (CH-53 Sea Stallion)*

*Sikorsky RH-53D.*

While some may read into that a plea for US Marine Corps acquisition of new aircraft for tactical electronic warfare, and for seizing control of the air, it should be read for what it is: a cold, objective statement of fact about modern war.

*This early model CH-53A Sea Stallion was the first of the heavy-lift helicopters to equip the US Marines. A test programme on this model proved its aerobatic ability in a series of carefully controlled rolls and loops.*

## A future for the service

In those few lines lie the roots of a profound question that US Marine Corps leadership must address soon. Is there any future need for a force geared to amphibious landings on Pacific islands? If there is, what kind of air elements should be organized and equipped? To make basic changes like that in the US Marine Corps will produce some trauma; but it may be the only way to guarantee the future existence of a proud service.

# The United States
# Air Force

**Though it usually enjoys a high standard of living on permanent bases with long concrete runways, which US Army and seagoing aircrew might envy, the US Air Force has to fly the longest global missions and, in emergency, up sticks and move the whole force to the other side of the globe in a matter of hours.**

There is a nice irony in the realization that most of the United States Air Force's combat aircraft now are dedicated to the single purpose of helping to win the war on the ground. It is ironic because for years the USAF fought bitterly against that mission, claiming that the real way to win a war was with strategic bombing of the enemy's industrial, fuel, power and transportation complexes. But thinking changed after a belated and realistic appraisal of the real-world situation of the 1970s. That appraisal was built on the postulate that 'small' wars will be the style, and that 'big' wars, especially the cataclysmic nuclear exchange, will be deterred.

The USAF has the awesome responsibility of two major tasks in that real-world environment: first, deterring the 'big' wars and, second, helping to win the 'small' ones.

The deterrent forces are in the hands of the Strategic Air Command (SAC), operators of the venerable Boeing B-52 Stratofortress, the controversial General Dynamics FB-111A, and a huge number of intercontinental ballistic missiles. The concept is that an enemy will not strike first if he

*With its barn-door speed-brake opened wide, this Eagle of the 49th TFW slows its roll-out on the runway at Holloman AFB.*

# Boeing B-52 Stratofortress

**SPECIFICATION**
**Boeing B-52H**
**Type:** long-range strategic bomber
**Powerplants:** eight 17,000-lb
(7711-kg) Pratt & Whitney TF33-P-3
turbofans
**Performance:** maximum speed Mach
0.95 or 630 mph (1014 km/h) at
40,000 ft (12192 m); typical cruising
speed 565 mph (909 km/h) at 36,000 ft
(10973 m); service ceiling 55,000 ft
(16764 m)
**Weight:** maximum take-off 505,000 lb
(229066 kg)
**Dimensions:** span 185 ft (56.39 m);
length 157 ft (47.85 m); height 40 ft 8 in
(12.4 m)
**Armament:** one T-171 20-mm gun in
General Electric rear gun position, 20
SRAM missiles (ALCM due to become
operational in the 1980s) and Quail
decoys

*Boeing B-52G in experimental three-colour upper surface camouflage.*

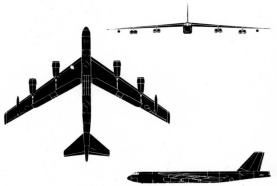

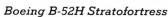

*Boeing B-52H Stratofortress*

*Boeing B-52H Stratofortress.*

knows that he will be smothered beneath a nuclear barrage of total, absolute, world-ending destruction. And since the United States is committed never to strike first (at least that is the current perception on the part of the general public), the presence of a powerful retaliatory force is supposed to guarantee that nuclear war will be deterred.

## Progressive but limited update

SAC's bomber force, particularly the 20-year-old B-52s, has been modernized and updated more times than can be tracked. A wealth of new electronic sensors and other equipment has been added to bring the capability of the big bombers up to match today's state of the art. Match, that is, in everything except aerodynamic performance. No amount of increased thrust or

*Escalation of price hit the F-111 before it really became fashionable. Secretary of Defense McNamara announced that SAC would get 210, but in the event the US Air Force could afford only 76 of these extremely potent but rather short-legged birds.*

# The United States Air Force

## General Dynamics F-111

*Tail-code NA identifies this General Dynamic:
F-111A as part of the 474th Tactical Fighter Wing
based at Nellis AFB, Nevada.*

# The United States Air Force

## General Dynamics F-111D cutaway drawing key

1 Hinged nose cone
2 Attack radar
3 Terrain-following radar
4 Nose hinges (2)
5 Radar mounting
6 Nose lock
7 Angle-of-sideslip probe
8 Homing antenna (high)
9 Forward warning antenna
10 Homing antenna (low and mid)
11 ALR-41 antenna
12 Flight control computers
13 Feel and trim assembly
14 Forward avionics bay (Advanced Mk II digital computer)
15 Angle-of-attack probe
16 UHF Comm/TACAN No 2
17 Module forward bulkhead and stabilization flaps (2)
18 Twin nosewheels
19 Shock strut
20 Underfloor impact attenuation bag stowage (4)
21 Nosewheel well
22 LOX converter
23 Rudder pedals
24 Control column
25 LOX heat exchanger
26 Auxiliary flotation bag pressure bottle
27 Weapons sight
28 Forward parachute bridle line
29 De-fog nozzle
30 Windscreen
31 Starboard console
32 Emergency oxygen bottles
33 Crew seats
34 Bulkhead console
35 Wing sweep control handle
36 Recovery chute catapult
37 Provision/survival pack
38 Attenuation bags pressure bottle
39 Recovery chute
40 Aft parachute bridle lined
41 UHF data link/AG IFF No. 1 (see 123)
42 Stabilization-brake chute
43 Self-righting bag
44 UHF recovery
45 ECM antennae (port and starboard)
46 Forward fuselage fuel bay
47 Ground re-fuelling receptable
48 Weapons bay
49 Module pitch flaps (port and starboard)
50 Aft flotation bag stowage
51 Aerial re-fuelling receptacle
52 Primary heat-exchanger (air-to-water)
53 Ram air inlet
54 Rate gyros
55 Rotating glove
56 Inlet variable spike
57 Port intake

58 Air brake/undercarriage door
59 Auxiliary inlet blow-in doors
60 Rotating glove pivot point
61 Inlet vortex generators
62 Wings sweep pivot
63 Wing centre-box assembly
64 Wing sweep actuator
65 Wing sweep feedback
66 Control runs
67 Rotating glove drive set
68 Inboard pivot pylons (2)
69 Auxiliary drop tanks (600 US gal/2271 litres)
70 Outboard fixed pylon(s); subsonic/jettisonable
71 Slat drive set
72 Wing fuel tank (389.2 US gal/1473 litres)
73 Leading-edge slat
74 Starboard navigation light
75 Flap drive set
76 Outboard spoiler actuator
77 Starboard spoilers
78 Inboard spoiler actuator
79 Flaps
80 Wing swept position
81 Auxiliary flap
82 Auxiliary flap actuator
83 Nuclear weapons and weapons control equipment package
84 Wing sweep/Hi Lift control box
85 Flap, slat and glove drive mechanism
86 Starboard engine bay
87 Yaw feel spring
88 Roll feel spring
89 Yaw trim actuator
90 Yaw damper servo
91 Roll stick position transducer

92 Pitch trim actuator (manual)
93 Roll damper servo
94 Pitch trim actuator (series)
95 Pitch feel spring
96 Pitch-roll mixer
97 Pitch damper servo
98 Pitch stick position transducer
99 Aft fuselage frames
100 Aft fuselage fuel bays

101 Horizontal stabilizer servo actuator
102 Starboard horizontal stabilizer
103 Aft warning antennae
104 HF antennae
105 Detector scanner
106 X-Band radar
107 Rudder
108 Integral vent tank

109 Fin aft spar
110 Fin structure
111 Fin/fuselage attachment
112 Rudder servo actuator
113 Variable nozzle
114 Tailfeathers
115 ECM antenna
116 ALR-41 antenna
117 Horizontal stabilizer structure

118 Horizontal stabilizer pivot point
119 Free floating blow-in doors
120 Afterburner section
121 Horizontal stabilizer servo actuator
122 Wing swept position
123 UHF data link/AG IFF No. 2
124 Ventral fin
125 Fire detection sensing element loops

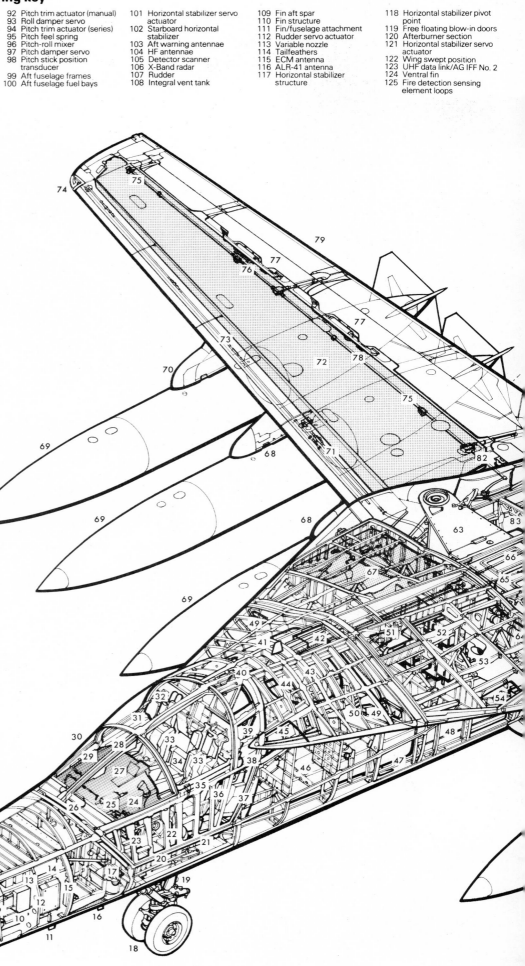

126 Cross frame
127 Engine access hatches
128 Engine accessories
129 Pratt and Whitney TF 30 turbofan
130 Three-stage fan
131 Intake duct
132 Fire extinguishing agent container and nozzles
133 Wing box skinning
134 Port mainwheel

135 Auxiliary drop tanks (600 US gal/2271 litres)
136 Pivot pylon
137 Pivot point
138 Pivot actuator
139 Flap tracks
140 Fixed pylon strong point
141 Outboard fixed jettisonable pylon
142 Wing integral fuel
143 Wing box structure
144 Port navigation light

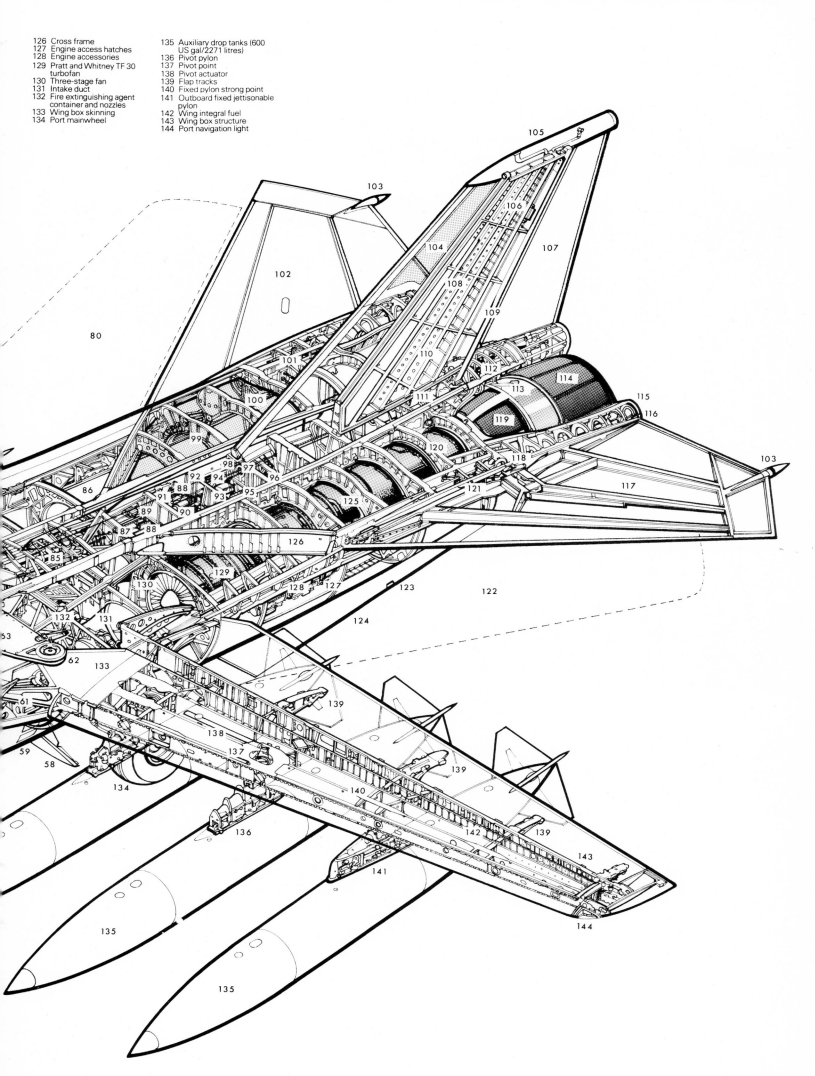

# The United States Air Force

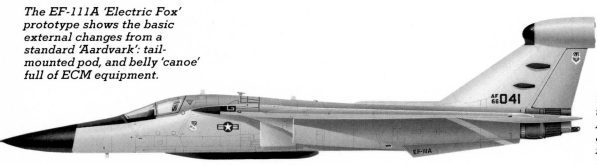

*The EF-111A 'Electric Fox' prototype shows the basic external changes from a standard 'Aardvark': tail-mounted pod, and belly 'canoe' full of ECM equipment.*

*The pods, knobs and bumps at the tail of this prototype EF-111A emphasize its role as a tactical jammer. It is a modified F-111 with the ALQ-99 ECM suite installed.*

# General Dynamics F-111

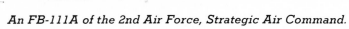

*An FB-111A of the 2nd Air Force, Strategic Air Command.*

## SPECIFICATION

**Type:** two-seat all-weather attack aircraft (F-111), electronic warfare aircraft (EF-111) and strategic bomber (FB-111)

**Powerplant:** two Pratt & Whitney TF30 afterburning turbofans: TF30-P-3s of 18,500-lb (8390-kg) static thrust in A and C; TF30-P-9s of 19,600-lb (8890-kg) static thrust in D and E; TF30-P-100s of 25,100-lb (11385-kg) static thrust in F; TF30-P-7s of 20,350-lb (9230-kg) static thrust in FB-111

**Performance:** maximum speed (clean) at 35,000 ft (10670 m) and above, Mach 2.2 (1,450 mph/2335 km/h); maximum speed (clean) at low level Mach 1.2 (800 mph/1287 km/h); range with internal and external fuel (A and C) 3,165 miles (5093 km); (F) more than 2,925 miles (4704 km); (EF) 2,416 miles (3889 km); service ceiling (clean) (A) 51,000 ft (15550 m), (F) 60,000 ft (18300 m), (EF) 50,000 ft (15250 m)

**Weights:** empty (A) 46,172 lb (20943 kg), (C) 47,300 lb (21455 kg), (D and E) about 49,000 lb (22226 kg), (F), 47,175 lb (21398 kg), (FB) about 50,000 lb (22680 kg), (EF) 53,600 lb (24313 kg)

**Dimensions:** span fully spread (A, D, E and F) 63 ft 0 in (19.20 m), (C and FB) 70 ft 0 in (21.34 m); span fully swept (A, D, E and F) 31 ft 11½ in (9.74 m), (C and FB) 33 ft 11 in (10.34 m); length 73 ft 6 in (22.40 m), (EF) 77 ft 0 in (23.47 m); height 17 ft 1½ in (5.22 m), (EF) 20 ft 0 in (6.10 m)

**Armament:** (F) two 750-lb (341-kg) B-43 bombs, or one 20-mm M61 multi-barrel cannon and one B-43 bomb, in internal weapons bay. All six wing points 'wet', for carriage or drop-tanks instead of weapons; maximum ordnance load (E) 29,000 lb (13154 kg), (FB) 37,500 lb (17010 kg) as fifty 750-lb (341-kg) bombs, two in internal bay and 48 on wing pylons

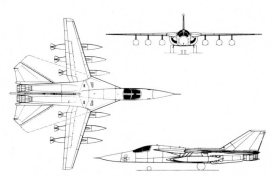

*General Dynamics FB-111A*

*Calculated to bring mixed feelings back to the guys who did it, the blasting water-injection take-offs of overloaded BUFFs from the slippery switchback runway at Guam were way outside the safety limits applied to civil operations. Ahead lies another nine-plus hours nothing like what the designer envisaged.*

added equipment is going to give the tired old 'Buff' a supersonic dash speed. That regime is reserved for the relatively small number of FB-111As operated by SAC. They remain the only aircraft in the USAF inventory that can make a blind first pass at a target in any weather, and most likely hit the mark dead centre.

Strategic Air Command also is the single manager for the USAF's 600-plus Boeing KC-135 tanker aircraft which fly on racetrack orbits located at key positions around the world, waiting and ready to refuel any aircraft capable of receiving. Almost one-quarter of the KC-135 fleet is operated by Air National Guard units, as part of the USAF concept for maintaining the readiness of the reserve forces.

In the early 1980s the administration of President Ronald Reagan asked for funding to put the

*An early model F-111A, wings set for long-endurance performance, loafs along below the photographer. The red-lined geometric figure aft of the cockpit identifies the refuelling receptacle.*

# Boeing KC-135

## SPECIFICATION

**Type:** turbine-powered tanker/transport
**Powerplant:** (KC-135A derivatives) four 13,500-lb (6124-kg) Pratt & Whitney J57-P-59W turbojets; (C-135B) four 18,000-lb (8165-kg) thrust Pratt & Whitney TF33-P-5 turbofans
**Performance:** (C-135B) maximum speed 600 mph (966 km/h); average cruising at 35,000 ft (10670 m) 530 mph (853 km/h)
**Weights:** (C-135B) operating empty 102,300 lb (46403 kg); maximum take-off 275,500 lb (124965 kg)
**Dimensions:** (KC-135A) span 130 ft 10 in (39.88 m); length 136 ft 3 in (41.53 m); height 38 ft 4 in (11.68 m); wing area 2,433 sq ft (226.03 m²)
**Armament:** none

*EC-135H airborne command post of C-in-C Europe (10th ACCS, Mildenhall).*

*Boeing KC-135 Stratotanker*

*Boeing KC-135 Stratotanker.*

Rockwell B-1 supersonic bomber into production. It was a gesture designed to impress the Russians and enrich American defence workers. Whether it will do either is a good question. The current thinking on the B-1, both in and out of the USAF, is that it may well be obsolete during the same year that it begins operations with SAC squadrons.

## TAC's new inventory

Tactical Air Command, the biggest element of the USAF, has armed for the dirty, close-in war of armoured vehicles and foot soldiers. During the 1970s TAC methodically developed a string of new aircraft with great capabilities. They began replacing the left-overs of the Vietnam war in the latter half of the 1970s and, as TAC enters the 1980s new aircraft form the preponderant

*Thanks to prolonged testing and development with the four B-1 flight articles the specification for the production B-1B has been greatly augmented, especially in fuel and avionics. Here the fourth prototype noses in to a tanker.*

# Boeing E-3A Sentry 'AWACS'

## SPECIFICATION

**Type:** airborne early-warning and command post aircraft

**Powerplant:** four 21,000-lb (9525-kg) Pratt & Whitney TF33-PW-100/100A turbofans

**Performance:** maximum speed 530 mph (853 km/h) at altitude; endurance 6 hours at a distance of 1,000 miles (1609 km) from base; service ceiling 40,000 ft (12192 m)

**Weights:** empty 172,000 lb (78019 kg); maximum take-off 325,000 lb (147419 kg)

**Dimensions:** span 145 ft 9 in (44.42 m); length 152 ft 11 in (46.61 m); height 42 ft 5 in (12.93 m); wing area 2,890 sq ft (268.5 m²)

**Armament:** none

*Boeing E-3A Sentry, one of 34 operated by the US Air Force.*

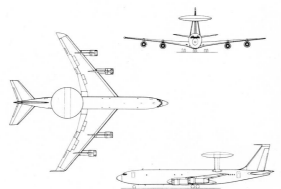

*Boeing E-3A Sentry (AWACS)*

*Boeing E-3A Sentry.*

portion of the fighting force.

TAC's new look was produced by the introduction of the McDonnell Douglas F-15A Eagle and the General Dynamics F-16A Fighting Falcon as a new generation of fighters, replacing the versatile, valuable but ageing McDonnell Douglas F-4 Phantom II. The close-support mission of tank- and bunker-busting was transferred to the Fairchild Republic A-10A Thunderbolt II (also known as the 'Warthog'). A special 'Wild Weasel' modification of the Phantom, the F-4G, has entered squadron service; its mission is the location and destruction of enemy missiles and other radar-directed weapons. General Dynamics F-111 tactical fighters, almost equal in capability to SAC bomber versions, continue to be the all-weather element of the strike force; but some of the earlier models of the type are being recycled through Grumman Aerospace to become tactical jamming and electronic-warfare aircraft under the designation of EF-111A. And over all these, in

*Another controversial military aircraft is the Boeing E-3A Sentry, popularly called the AWACS (Airborne Warning and Control System). It's intended to be the 'sky boss' of an air/ground battle, working from a God's-eye view to orchestrate both offensive and defensive moves.*

# The United States Air Force

*There are a lot of things going on in camouflage these days, and this is probably a temporary scheme for F-15s based in, or deployed to, a desert area.*

the sense of command and control, soars the stately Boeing E-3A Sentry, the airborne warning and control system (AWACS).

## Rejuvenated air defence

TAC's responsibilities increased late in the 1970s when it took over the operation of what had been the Aerospace Defense Command. ADC, with its force of 20-year-old General·Dynamics F-106A Delta Darts, seemed to be a withering force that needed an injection of something to restore it to health. It got the dosage, in the form of a TAC take-over. It was a move at first resented by veterans of the force; later it was appreciated and even applauded as the only way to go. ADTAC (Air Defense, Tactical Air Command) now is a rejuvenated organization, and its antique interceptors are being phased out in favour of new F-15s.

TAC is a quick-reaction force, designed to be deployed rapidly to reinforce fighter and attack squadrons on bases in Europe and the Pacific with the United States Air Forces Europe (USAFE) and the Pacific Air Forces (PACAF) respectively. It is a simple concept; not knowing

*What you do is take the finest interceptor and hang conformal tanks on it plus a lot of bombs and some other systems, add a second crewman to handle the knobs and switches, and you have an instant ground-attack aircraft. This is the Strike Eagle version of the elegant F-15B/D two-seater.*

# McDonnell Douglas F-15 Eagle

## SPECIFICATION

**Type:** single-seat air-superiority fighter

**Powerplant:** two Pratt & Whitney F100-PW-100 turbofan engines, each of 23,800-lb (10976-kg) thrust with afterburning

**Performance:** maximum speed 921 mph (1482 km/h) at low altitude, Mach 2.5 at altitude; maximum radius of action, 2,878 miles (4631 km) with three 600 US gallon tanks; maximum rate of climb 40,000 ft/min (12192 m/min); service ceiling 63,000 ft (19203 m)

**Weights:** empty 28,000 lb (12700 kg); maximum take-off 56,000 lb (25401 kg)

**Dimensions:** span 42 ft 10 in (13.05 m); length 63 ft 9 in (19.43 m); height 18 ft 8 in (5.63 m); wing area 608 sq ft (56.5 m²)

**Armament:** one 20-mm M61A-1 rotating-barrel gun and up to eight air-to-air missiles (normally four AIM-7F Sparrow III and four AIM-9L Sidewinder) under guidance of APG-63 pulsed-Doppler radar with search range of 150 miles (240 km)

*An early F-15A of the 58th TFTW, Luke AFB, Arizona.*

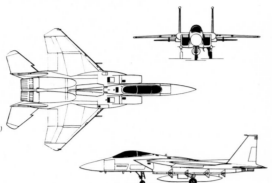

*McDonnell Douglas F-15A Eagle.*

*McDonnell Douglas F-15A Eagle.*

where war might break out, and knowing full well that the first few days will be critical to the outcome, TAC plans to deploy squadron-sized reinforcements to any location in the world, and to have them ready to fight literally within minutes after their arrival.

Within the command, some squadrons are actually dual-based; they rotate between a foreign base and a home base, maintaining currency in the environment where they may have to fight. Other squadrons are designated as quick reactors, and maintain a state of readiness that is tested with frequent deployments and exercises within the United States and abroad. There is one technical point of command that needs to be appreciated, though. When a squadron leaves its TAC base for a foreign location, it will come under the command of either USAFE or PACAF about halfway across. Consequently, TAC is not a combat command; it is a training command, although you do not say that too loudly in any TAC ready room. TAC furnishes the fighter pilots

*Once the USAF decided that air-superiority blue was a failure as a combat colour, cooler heads prevailed and this two-tone low-visibility grey was applied to the F-15s.*

# McDonnell Douglas F-15A Eagle

HOLLOMAN'S EAGLE

*The commander of the 49th Tactical Fighter Wing, Holloman AFB, New Mexico, piloted this F-15A. How many strings were pulled to get a serial number ending in 49?*

## McDonnell Douglas F-15C Eagle cutaway drawing key

1 Tailplane honeycomb construction
2 Boron fibre skin panel
3 Tailplane spars
4 All-moving tailplane pivot fixing
5 Leading edge dog-tooth
6 Low-voltage formation lighting strip
7 Fin root attachment frames
8 Rudder hydraulic rotary actuator
9 Rudder honeycomb construction
10 Fin spar construction
11 Boron fibre skin panel
12 Anti-collision light
13 Electronic counter-measures aerials (ECM)
14 Variable area afterburner exhaust nozzles
15 Nozzle sealing flaps
16 Fueldraulic nozzle actuators
17 Afterburner duct
18 Engine bay titanium ring frames
19 Rear engine mounting frame
20 Engine bay titanium frame and stringer construction
21 Titanium skin panelling
22 Port tailplane hydraulic actuator
23 Tailplane hinge arm
24 Port rudder
25 Tailboom fairing
26 ECM aerial
27 Port tailplane
28 Tail navigation light
29 ECM aerial
30 Radar warning aerials
31 Boron fibre skin panelling
32 Fin leading edge
33 Port air system equipment bay

34 Forward engine mounting
35 Engine mounting frame
36 Bleed air system ducting
37 Engine support link
38 Engine bay fireproof bulkhead
39 Pratt & Whitney F100-PW-100 afterburning turbofan engine
40 Starboard air system equipment bay
41 Engine bleed air primary heat exchanger
42 Heat exchanger ventral exhaust duct
43 Retractable runway arrester hook

44 Wing trailing edge fuel tank
45 Flap hydraulic jack
46 Starboard plain flap
47 Flap and aileron honeycomb panel construction
48 Starboard aileron
49 Aileron hydraulic actuator
50 Fuel jettison pipe
51 Aluminium honeycomb wing tip fairing
52 Low-voltage formation lighting
53 Starboard navigation light
54 ECM aerial
55 Westinghouse ECM equipment pod

56 Outboard wing stores pylon
57 Pylon attachment spigot
58 Cambered leading edge ribs
59 Front spar
60 Machined wing skin/stringer panels
61 Outboard pylon fixing
62 HF flush aerial
63 Leading edge fuel tank
64 Inboard pylon fixing
65 Wing rib construction
66 Starboard wing integral fuel tank, total internal fuel load, 13,455-lb (6103-kg)
67 Wing root rib support struts
68 Titanium wing spars
69 Wing spar/fuselage attachment pin joints
70 Machined fuselage main bulkheads
71 Wing/fuselage fuel tank interconnections
72 Airframe mounted engine accessory gearbox
73 Standby hydraulic generator

74 Jet fuel starter (JFS)/auxiliary power unit (APU)
75 Engine intake compressor face
76 Cooling system intake bleed air spill duct
77 Port wing trailing edge fuel tank
78 Port plain flap
79 Flap hydraulic jack
80 Aileron control rod
81 Aileron hydraulic actuator
82 Port aileron

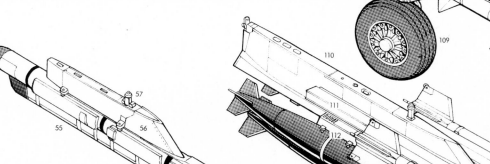

# Modern American Combat Aircraft

*One of the great drawbacks of the F-15 is its size; fighter pilots call it 'The Magnet' for obvious reasons. If you could confuse enemy pilots about which way you were turning, you might have an advantage. That was the thinking behind this deceptive camouflage scheme developed by artist Keith Ferris.*

83 Fuel jettison pipe
84 Wing tip fairing
85 Low-voltage formation lighting
86 Port navigation light
87 ECM aerial
88 Cambered leading edge
89 Outboard pylon fixing
90 Port wing internal fuel tank
91 Fuel system piping
92 Inboard pylon fixing
93 Leading edge fuel tank
94 Anti-collision light
95 Boom-type air refuelling receptacle
96 Bleed air duct to air conditioning plant
97 Control rod runs
98 Dorsal airbrake, open
99 Airbrake glass-fibre honeycomb construction
100 Airbrake hydraulic jack
101 Centre fuselage fuel tanks
102 Intake ducting
103 Ammunition feed chute
104 M61A-1 Vulcan 20-mm cannon
105 Hydraulic rotary cannon drive unit
106 Starboard anti-collision light
107 Ventral main undercarriage wheel bay
108 Main undercarriage leg strut
109 Starboard mainwheel
110 Inboard stores pylon
111 Air-to-air missile adaptor
112 Bomb rack
113 Mk 82 low drag 500-lb (227-kg) HE bombs
114 Bomb triple ejector rack
115 Missile launch rail
116 AIM-9L Sidewinder air-to-air missile
117 AIM-7F Sparrow air-to-air missile
118 Sparrow missile launcher unit
119 Cannon muzzle aperture
120 Cannon barrels
121 Central ammunition drum, 940-rounds
122 Airbrake hinges
123 Forward fuselage fuel tanks
124 UHF aerial
125 Intake duct bleed air louvres
126 Intake by-pass air spill duct
127 Variable area intake ramp hydraulic actuator
128 Air conditioning system cooling air exhaust duct
129 Canopy hinge point
130 Air conditioning plant
131 Intake incidence control jack
132 Intake duct variable area ramp doors
133 Intake pivot fixing
134 Starboard engine air intake
135 Nosewheel leg door
136 Nose undercarriage leg strut
137 Nosewheel
138 Landing/taxying lamps
139 Nosewheel retraction strut
140 Rear underfloor equipment bay
141 Tactical electronic warfare system (TEWS) racks
142 Cockpit coaming
143 Rear pressure bulkhead
144 Canopy jack
145 Cockpit pressurization valves
146 Structural space provision for second crew member (F-15D)
147 Cockpit aft decking
148 Canopy arch
149 Port intake external compression lip
150 Fuel and sensor tactical (FAST) pack, conformal fuel pallet, capacity 5,000-lb (2268-kg)
151 600-US gal (2270-litre) external fuel tank
152 Cockpit canopy cover
153 Ejection seat headrest
154 Seat safety handle/arming lever
155 Canopy emergency jettison linkage
156 Ejection seat launch rails
157 Safety harriess
158 McDonnell-Douglas ACES II 'zero-zero' ejection seat
159 Cockpit sloping bulkhead
160 Pilots side console panel
161 Air conditioning ducting
162 Forward underfloor equipment bay, built-in test equipment (BITE) and liquid oxygen converter
163 Low-voltage formation lighting strip
164 Port side retractable boarding ladder
165 TACAN aerial
166 Angle of attack probe
167 Rudder pedals
168 Control column
169 Pilot's head-up display (HUD)
170 Instrument panel shroud
171 Frameless windscreen panel
172 ADF sense aerial
173 Radio and electronics equipment bay, port and starboard
174 Cockpit front pressure bulkhead
175 Pitot tube
176 UHF aerial
177 Radar mounting bulkhead
178 Radome hinge mounting
179 ILS aerial
180 Radar scanner mounting and tracking mechanism
181 Hughes APG-63 pulse doppler radar scanner
182 Scanner mounted IFF aerial array
183 Glass-fibre radome

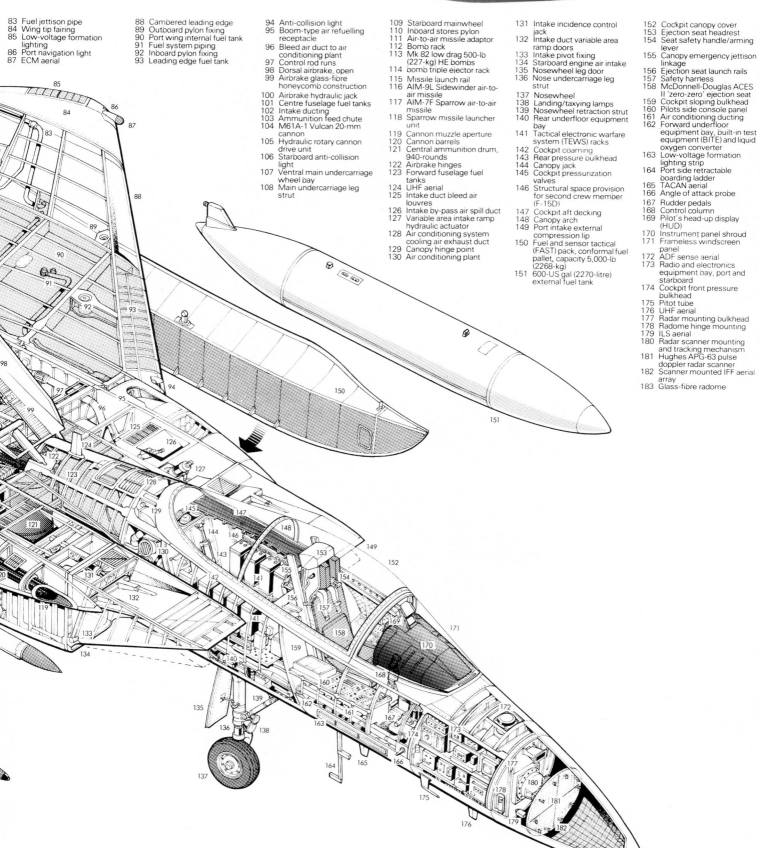

# General Dynamics F-16 Fighting Falcon

*Once upon a time, the F-16A was thought of
as an inexpensive fighter, but not so any longer.
Now the cost of buying an incomplete
aeroplane comes out. But at least you get a
versatile warplane for the money. This one
carries Sidewinders so that it can fight, tanks
so that it can get somewhere, and bombs to
drop after it gets there.*

## General Dynamics F-16 cutaway drawing key

1. Pitot tube
2. Glassfibre radome
3. Planar radar scanner
4. ILS glidescope aerial
5. Scanner drive units
6. Radar mounting bulkhead
7. ADF aerial
8. Forward electronics equipment bay
9. Westinghouse AN/APG-66 digital pulse doppler radar electronics
10. Forward identification light, Danish and Norwegian aircraft only
11. Radar warning antenna
12. Cockpit front pressure bulkhead
13. Instrument panel shroud
14. Weapons systems fire control electronics
15. Fuselage forebody strake fairing
16. Marconi-Elliot wide-angle raster-video head-up-display (WARHUD)
17. Side stick controller (fly-by-wire control system)
18. Cockpit floor
19. Frameless bubble canopy
20. Canopy fairing
21. McDonnell-Douglas ACES II zero-zero ejection seat
22. Pilot's safety harness
23. Engine throttle
24. Side console panel
25. Cockpit frame construction
26. Rear pressure bulkhead
27. Ejection seat headrest
28. Seat arming safety lever
29. Cockpit sealing frame
30. Canopy hinge point
31. Ejection launch rails
32. Rear electronics equipment bay (growth area)
33. Boundary layer splitter plate
34. Fixed geometry engine air intake
35. Lower UHF/IFF aerial
36. Aft retracting nosewheel
37. Shock absorber scissor links
38. Retraction strut
39. Nosewheel door
40. Forward position light
41. Intake trunking
42. Cooling air louvres
43. Gun gas suppression nozzle
44. Air conditioning system piping
45. Forward fuselage fuel tank, total system capacity 1,072.5 US gal (4058 litres)
46. Canopy aft glazing
47. Starboard 370 US gal external fuel tank (1400 litres)
48. Forebody blended wing root
49. Upper position light and flight refuelling floodlight
50. Fuel tank bay access panel

51. Rotary cannon barrels
52. Forebody frame construction
53. M-61 Vulcan, 20-mm rotary cannon
54. Ammunition feed and link return chutes
55. Ammunition drum, 500-rounds
56. Ammunition drum flexible drive shaft
57. Hydraulic gun drive motor
58. Leading-edge flap control shaft
59. Hydraulic equipment service bay
60. Primary system hydraulic reservoir
61. Leading-edge manoeuvre flap drive motor
62. TACAN aerial
63. No.2 hydraulic system reservoir
64. Leading-edge flap control shaft
65. Inboard pylon
66. Pylon fixing
67. Wing centre pylon
68. Triple ejector bomb rack
69. MK 82 500-lb (227-kg) bombs
70. Oldelft Orpheus reconnaissance pod, Netherlands aircraft only
71. Infra-red linescan
72. Camera ports
73. Reconnaissance pod pylon adaptor, centre link fixing
74. SUU-25E/A flare launcher
75. AN/ASQ aircraft instrumentation system data link transmitter
76. Outboard wing pylon

77. Missile launch shoe
78. AIM-9L Sidewinder air-to-air missile
79. Advanced medium range air-to-air missile (AMRAAM)
80. Aluminium honeycomb leading-edge flap
81. Starboard navigation light
82. Static dischargers
83. Fixed trailing edge section
84. Multi-spar wing construction
85. Integral wing fuel tank
86. Starboard flaperon
87. Fuel system piping
88. Access panels
89. Centre fuel tank bay access panel
90. Intake ducting
91. Wing mounting bulkheads
92. Universal air refuelling receptacle (UARSSI)
93. Engine compressor face
94. Pratt & Whitney F100-PW-100(3) afterburning turbofan engine
95. Jet fuel starter
96. Engine accessory gearbox, airframe mounted
97. Gearbox drive shaft
98. Ground pressure refuelling receptacle
99. Flaperon servo actuator
100. Rear fuselage frame construction

101. Rear integral fuel tank
102. Main engine mounting suspension link
103. Upper UHF/IFF aerial
104. Fuselage skin plating
105. Starboard side-body fairing
106. Fin root fillet
107. Flight control system hydraulic accumulators
108. Anti-collision light power supply unit
109. Starboard tailplane (increased area 'big tail')
110. Tailplane surfaces interchangeable port and starboard
111. Graphite-epoxy skin panels
112. Fin construction
113. Aluminium honeycomb leading-edge panel
114. Steel leading-edge strip
115. VHF communications aerial
116. Anti-collision light
117. Tail radar warning antennae

118. Aluminium honeycomb rudder construction
119. Rudder servo actuator
120. Radar warning power supply
121. Brake parachute housing, Norwegian aircraft only
122. Tail navigation light
123. Electronic counter-measures aerials, port and starboard (ECM)
124. Fully variable exhaust nozzle
125. Nozzle flaps
126. Split trailing edge airbrake, upper and lower surfaces
127. Airbrake hydraulic jack
128. Port tailplane (increased area 'big tail')
129. Static dischargers
130. Graphite-epoxy tailplane skin panels
131. Corrugated aluminium substructure
132. Hinge pivot fixing
133. Tailplane servo actuator
134. Nozzle sealing fairing

135. Fueldraulic nozzle actuators
136. Afterburner tailpipe
137. Rear fuselage bulkheads
138. Rear engine mounting
139. Aft position light
140. Port side-body fairing
141. Runway arrester hook
142. Ventral fin, port and starboard
143. Port flaperon
144. Flaperon hinges
145. Aluminium honeycomb flaperon construction
146. Static dischargers
147. Fixed trailing edge section
148. Port AIM-9L Sidewinder air-to-air missiles
149. Missile launcher shoe
150. Wing tip launcher fixing
151. Port navigation light
152. Outboard pylon fixing rib
153. Multi-spar wing construction
154. Centre pylon attachment rib
155. Wing centre pylon

*The Wolf Pack, Pacific Air Forces' 8th Tactical Fighter Wing, is based at Kunsan Air Base in South Korea. This is one of the F-16As that now equip the unit.*

156 MK 84 2,000-lb (980-kg) low-drag bomb
157 Leading-edge manoeuvre flap
158 Leading-edge flap rotary actuators
159 Integral wing fuel tank
160 Inboard pylon fixing
161 Wing attachment fishplates
162 Landing/taxiing lamp
163 Main undercarriage shock absorber strut
164 Mainwheel leg strut
165 Retraction strut

166 Mainwheel door
167 Forward retracting mainwheel
168 Port underwing fuel tank, 370 US gal (1700 litres)
169 Centre line external fuel tank, 300 US gal (1378 litres)
170 Electro-optical forward looking infra-red pod (EO-FLIR)
171 Laser target designator pod (LAST)

172 LAU-3/A rocket launcher, 19x2.75-in (6.98-cm) ground attack rockets
173 Westinghouse AN/ALQ119-1 electronic suppression system radar jamming pod (ESM)
174 Snakeye, 500-lb (227-kg) retarded bomb
175 GBU-10C/B, 2,000-lb (908-kg) laser guided bomb

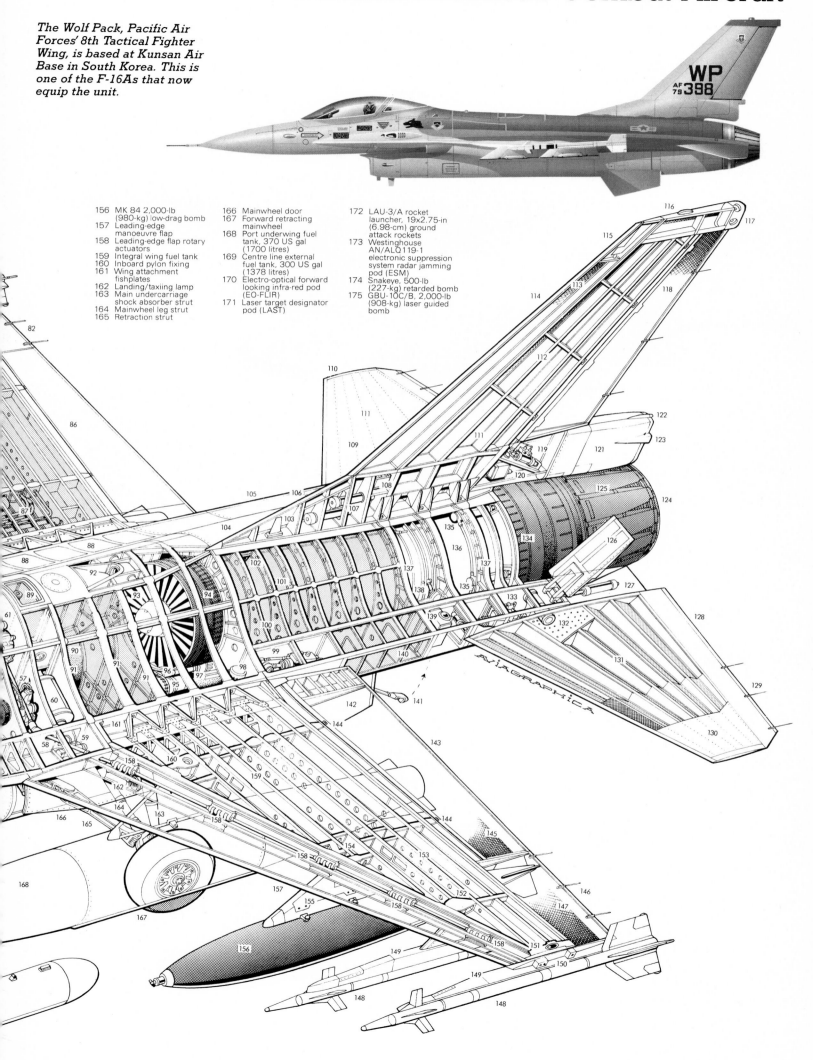

and aircraft for worldwide deployment and combat and, to meet that imposing requirement, trains its pilots in the most realistic and demanding exercises that can be devized.

*Four of the 388th TFW's F-16As, one from each of the four squadrons in the wing, form up for the camera.*

## Small war exercise

The reasoning that lies behind the TAC dictum to train as you would fight stems from studies of the successes and failures of earlier air combat. Those studies, conducted after both world wars and the Vietnam conflict, showed that the majority of the fighter pilots who were lost in combat were downed before they had completed 10 missions. Put another way, once a fighter pilot had completed 10 missions, his chances of survival zoomed remarkably.

In that case, thought some TAC leaders, why not give pilots their first 10 combat sorties in a

# General Dynamics F-16

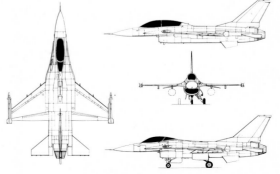

### SPECIFICATION
**Type:** single-seat tactical fighter (F-16A) and two-seat combat trainer (F-16B)
**Powerplant:** one 23,810-lb (10800-kg) Pratt & Whitney F100-PW-200 afterburning turbofan
**Performance:** maximum speed 914 mph (1455 km/h) or Mach 1.2 at sea level, and 1,320+ mph (2124+ km/h) or Mach 2 at altitude; initial climb rate 60,000+ ft/min (18288+ m/min); service ceiling about 60,000 ft (18288 m); combat radius 575 miles (925 km); ferry range with drop tanks 2,303 miles (3705 km)
**Weights:** (F-16A) operational empty 14,567 lb (6607 kg); internal fuel 6,972 lb (3162 kg); maximum external load 15,200 lb (6894 kg); design take-off gross, clean 22,500 lb (10205 kg); maximum take-off without external tanks 22,785 lb (10335 kg), with external load 37,500 lb (17,010 kg)
**Dimensions:** span (over missiles) 32 ft 10 in (10.01 m); length 47 ft 7¾ in (14.52 m); height 16 ft 5¼ in (5.01 m); wing area 300 sq ft (27.87 m²)
**Armament:** one 20-mm General Electric

*F-16A Fighting Falcon of 388th TFW, Hill AFB, Utah.*

M61A-1 multi-barrel cannon in left wing/body fairing, with 500 rounds; one AIM-9J/L Sidewinder infra-red homing missile at each wingtip (radar-homing Sparrow or AMRAAM later) for air-to-air interception; six underwing hardpoints and one under fuselage for up to 15,200 lb (6894 kg) of attack weapons or drop-tanks (10,500 lb/4763 kg if full internal fuel is carried). Stores under wings/fuselage can include four more Sidewinders or Sparrows, Pave Penny laser tracking pod, single or cluster bombs, flare pods, air-to-surface missiles, laser-guided and electro-optical weapons

*F-16A Fighting Falcon (upper side view: F-16B)*

# Fairchild A-10 Thunderbolt II

## SPECIFICATION

**Type:** single-seat close support/anti-tank bomber

**Powerplant:** two General Electric TF34-GE-100 high-bypass turbofans, each of 9,065-lb (4112-kg) thrust

**Performance:** nominal cruise speed (no external stores) 345 kg 397 mph/640 km/h ; design maximum speed, 518 mph/722 km/h ; take-off roll (maximum weight) 3,800 ft (1158 m); loiter endurance (250 nautical miles from base, 18 Mk82 bombs and 750 rounds of GAU-8 ammunition), 2 hours

**Weights:** operating empty (aircraft ready to fly, less fuel, ammunition and pilot) 24,000 lb (10866 kg); maximum external payload (full internal fuel) 11,980 lb (5434 kg); maximum payload (with partial fuel) 16,000 lb (7258 kg)

**Dimensions:** span 57 ft 6 in (17.53 m); length 54 ft 4 in (16.26 m); height 14 ft 8 in (4.47 m); wing area 506 sq ft (47.01 m²)

**Armament:** one 30-mm rotating-barrel gun plus various combinations of external stores

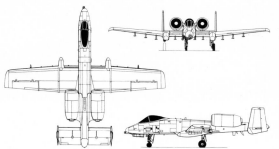

*A-10A in experimental camouflage with the 57th Fighter Weapons Wing, Tactical Air Command, Nellis AFB.*

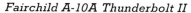

*Fairchild A-10A Thunderbolt II*

*Fairchild A-10A Thunderbolt II.*

*The current final camouflage scheme of the Thunderbolt II is called 'European I', and features two shades of green and one of dark grey. This aircraft is on the roster of the 354th Tactical Fighter Wing, Myrtle Beach, South Carolina.*

free-form exercise environment, where they do everything except actually shoot down their opposition That idea germinated into 'Red Flag', a wide-ranging air war staged at regularly scheduled intervals over the barren Nevada desert country north and west of Nellis Air Force Base, near Las Vegas. Each 'Red Flag' exercise sets up some kind of a 'small war' situation, with a reasonable scenario and a solid reason for the employment of air power. Strike forces are tasked, launched and harassed on the way by USAF 'aggressors' flying Northrop F-5Es which simulate the Russian Mikoyan-Gurevich MiG-21 radar and visual signatures. Near the target sites are batteries of simulated anti-aircraft artillery and missiles, the realism augmented even further by smoke trails from fancy fireworks. The sounds, sights and sweat of real combat are closely duplicated in these air wars, and many a fighter pilot has been momentarily terrified as he glances over his shoulder and sees a red-starred fighter slipping into the killing position at six o'clock.

# Fairchild A-10 Thunderbolt II

*Face it, Fairchild: it really doesn't look good from any angle. But the A-10A can belly along through weeds, it hauls a lot of ordnance and pilots love to fly it fast and low.*

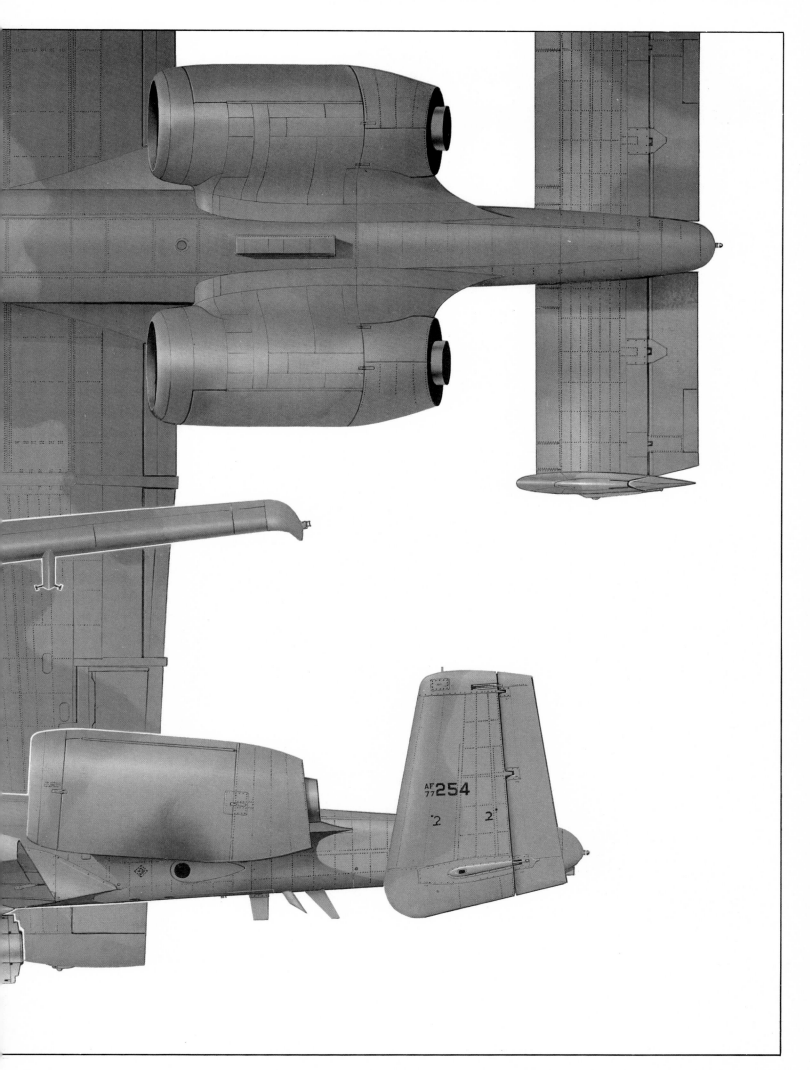

AF
77 254

# The United States Air Force

While the second prototype YA-10A was being evaluated in spin tests at Edwards AFB, it carried white areas on outboard tail and wing panels to improve photographic coverage. The striped nose boom carries test sensors.

Evaluation of night and adverse-weather systems was done in this two-seat modification of a leased A-10A. New sensor systems included forward-looking infra-red, low-light-level TV, and radar; an inertial navigation system also was installed.

## Fairchild A-10A Thunderbolt II cutaway drawing key

1 Cannon muzzles
2 Nose cap
3 ILS aerial
4 Air-to-air refuelling receptacle (open)
5 Nosewheel bay (offset to starboard)
6 Cannon barrels
7 Rotary cannon barrel bearing
8 Gun compartment ventilating intake
9 L-band radar warning aerial
10 Electrical system relay switches
11 Windscreen rain dispersal air duct
12 Pave Penny laser search and tracking pod
13 Windscreen panel
14 Head-up display symbol generator
15 Pilot's head-up display screen
16 Instrument panel shroud
17 Air-to-air refuelling pipe
18 Titanium armour cockpit enclosure
19 Rudder pedals
20 Battery
21 General Electric GAU-8/A 30-mm seven-barrelled rotary cannon
22 Ammunition feed ducts
23 Steering cylinder
24 Nose undercarriage leg strut
25 Nosewheel
26 Nosewheel scissor links
27 Retractable boarding ladder
28 Ventilating air outlets
29 Ladder stowage box
30 Pilot's side console panel
31 Engine throttles
32 Control column
33 McDonnell Douglas ACES 2 ejection seat
34 Headrest canopy breakers
35 Cockpit canopy cover
36 Canopy hinge mechanism
37 Space provision for additional avionics
38 Angle-of-attack probe
39 Emergency canopy release handle
40 Ventral access panels to gun compartment
41 Ammunition drum (1,350 rounds)
42 Ammunition drum armour plating
43 Electrical system servicing panel
44 Ventral fin
45 Spent cartridge-case return chute
46 Control cable runs
47 Avionics compartments
48 Forward/centre fuselage joint bulkhead
49 Aerial selector switches
50 IFF aerial
51 Anti-collision light
52 UHF/TACAN aerial
53 Starboard wing integral fuel tank
54 Wing skin plating
55 Outer wing panel attachment joint strap
56 Starboard fixed wing pylons

57 ALE-37A chaff dispenser pod
58 ALE/ALQ-119 electronic countermeasures pod
59 Pitot tube
60 Starboard drooped wing tip fairing
61 Split aileron/deceleron mass balance
62 Deceleron open position
63 Starboard aileron/deceleron
64 Deceleron hydraulic jack
65 Aileron hydraulic jack
66 Control linkages
67 Aileron tab
68 Tab balance weight
69 Slotted trailing edge flaps
70 Outboard flap jack
71 Flap synchronizing shafts
72 Fuselage self-sealing fuel cells (maximum internal fuel capacity 10,700 lb/ 4853 kg)
73 Fuselage main longeron
74 Longitudinal control and services duct
75 Air conditioning supply duct
76 Wing attaching fuselage main frames
77 Gravity fuel filler caps
78 Engine pylon fairing
79 Pylon attachment joint
80 Starboard intake
81 Intake centre cone
82 Engine fan blades

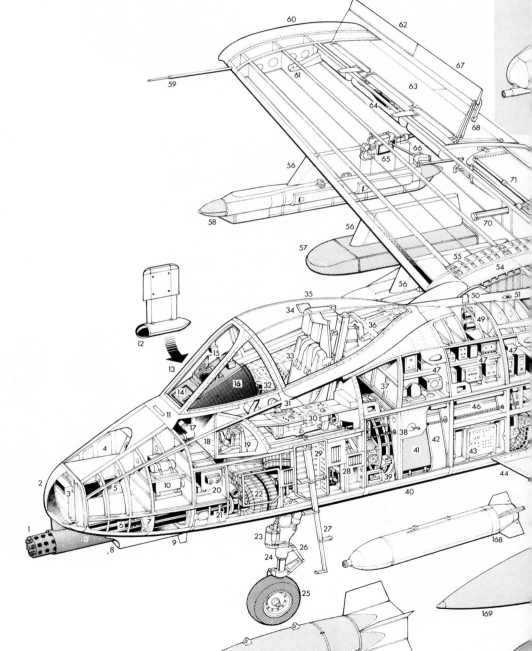

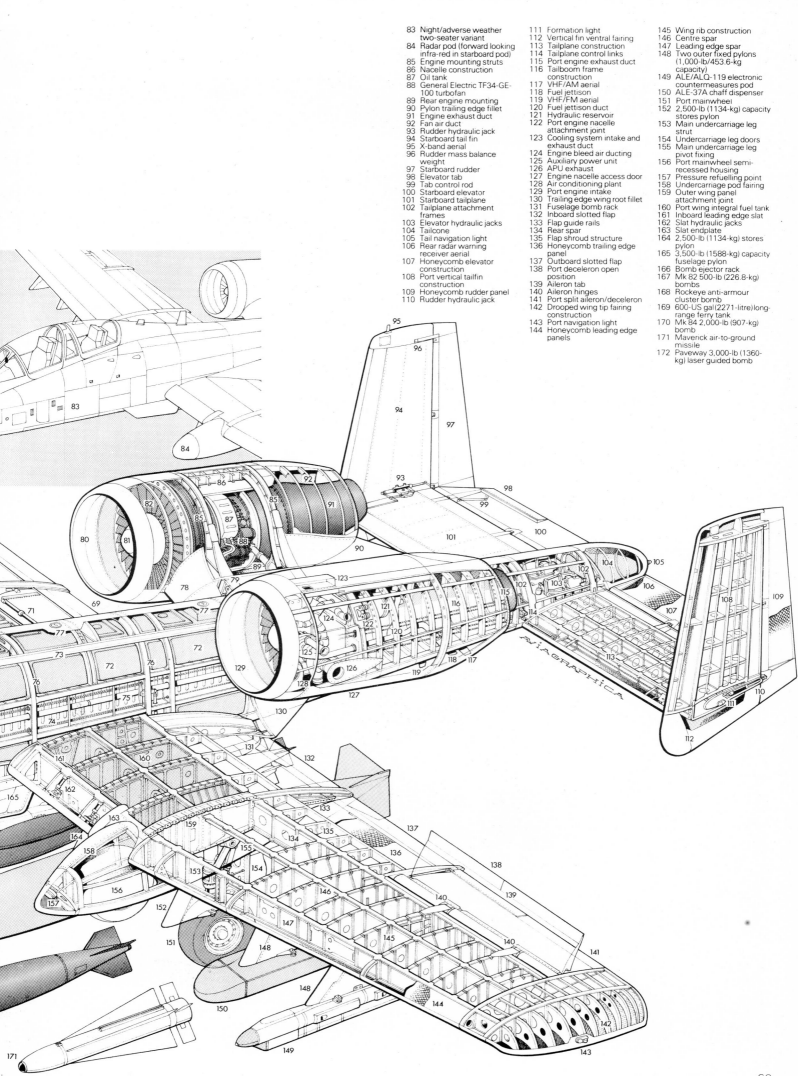

83 Night/adverse weather two-seater variant
84 Radar pod (forward looking infra-red in starboard pod)
85 Engine mounting struts
86 Nacelle construction
87 Oil tank
88 General Electric TF34-GE-100 turbofan
89 Rear engine mounting
90 Pylon trailing edge fillet
91 Engine exhaust duct
92 Fan air duct
93 Rudder hydraulic jack
94 Starboard tail fin
95 X-band aerial
96 Rudder mass balance weight
97 Starboard rudder
98 Elevator tab
99 Tab control rod
100 Starboard elevator
101 Starboard tailplane
102 Tailplane attachment frames
103 Elevator hydraulic jacks
104 Tailcone
105 Tail navigation light
106 Rear radar warning receiver aerial
107 Honeycomb elevator construction
108 Port vertical tailfin construction
109 Honeycomb rudder panel
110 Rudder hydraulic jack

111 Formation light
112 Vertical fin ventral fairing
113 Tailplane construction
114 Tailplane control links
115 Port engine exhaust duct
116 Tailboom frame construction
117 VHF/AM aerial
118 Fuel jettison
119 VHF/FM aerial
120 Fuel jettison duct
121 Hydraulic reservoir
122 Port engine nacelle attachment joint
123 Cooling system intake and exhaust duct
124 Engine bleed air ducting
125 Auxiliary power unit
126 APU exhaust
127 Engine nacelle access door
128 Air conditioning plant
129 Port engine intake
130 Trailing edge wing root fillet
131 Fuselage bomb rack
132 Inboard slotted flap
133 Flap guide rails
134 Rear spar
135 Flap shroud structure
136 Honeycomb trailing edge panel
137 Outboard slotted flap
138 Port deceleron open position
139 Aileron tab
140 Aileron hinges
141 Port split aileron/deceleron
142 Drooped wing tip fairing construction
143 Port navigation light
144 Honeycomb leading edge panels

145 Wing rib construction
146 Centre spar
147 Leading edge spar
148 Two outer fixed pylons (1,000-lb/453.6-kg capacity)
149 ALE/ALQ-119 electronic countermeasures pod
150 ALE-37A chaff dispenser
151 Port mainwheel
152 2,500-lb (1134-kg) capacity stores pylon
153 Main undercarriage leg strut
154 Undercarriage leg doors
155 Main undercarriage leg pivot fixing
156 Port mainwheel semi-recessed housing
157 Pressure refuelling point
158 Undercarriage pod fairing
159 Outer wing panel attachment joint
160 Port wing integral fuel tank
161 Inboard leading edge slat
162 Slat hydraulic jacks
163 Slat endplate
164 2,500-lb (1134-kg) stores pylon
165 3,500-lb (1588-kg) capacity fuselage pylon
166 Bomb ejector rack
167 Mk 82 500-lb (226.8-kg) bombs
168 Rockeye anti-armour cluster bomb
169 600-US gal (2271-litre) long-range ferry tank
170 Mk 84 2,000-lb (907-kg) bomb
171 Maverick air-to-ground missile
172 Paveway 3,000-lb (1360-kg) laser guided bomb

# McDonnell Douglas F-4 Phantom II

**SPECIFICATION**

**Type:** (F-4E) two-seat shipboard/land-based multi-role fighter/strike aircraft

**Powerplant:** two 17,900-lb (8127-kg) General Electric J79-GE-17 afterburning turbojets

**Performance:** maximum design speed (clean) Mach 2.17 or 1,430 mph (2304 km/h) at 36,000 ft (10973 m); cruising speed with full internal fuel, four AIM-7E missiles and two 308-gallon (1400 litre) drop tanks 572 mph (924 km/h) at 33,000 ft (10050 m); typical combat radius on hi-lo-hi mission with two 308-gallon (1400-litre) drop tanks and four AIM-7E missiles 520 miles (840 km); ferry range 1,610 miles (2593 km); service ceiling (clean) 58,750 ft (17907 m); maximum rate of climb (clean) 49,800 ft (15179 m) per minute

**Weights:** empty equipped 31,853 lb (14461 kg); normal take-off (internal fuel, four AIM-7E missiles and two 308-gallon/1400 litre drop tanks) 53,814 lb (24430 kg); maximum take-off 61,795 lb (28055 kg)

**Dimensions:** span 38 ft 4 in (11.68 m);

*F-4E of 32nd TFS, Camp Amsterdam, Netherlands (now an F-15 unit).*

length 63 ft 0 in (19.20 m); height 16 ft 5 in (5.00 m); wing area 530 sq ft (49.24 m²)

**Armament:** one 20-mm M61A1 rotary cannon with 640 rounds, four AIM 7E Sparrow missiles semi-recessed under fuselage, or up to 3,020 lb (1371 kg) on centreline pylon, plus various combinations of missiles and stores on four wing pylons up to a weight of 12,980 lb (5888 kg)

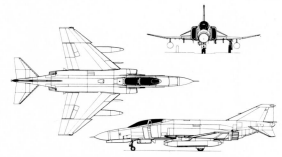

*McDonnell Douglas F-4E Phantom II*

It is not exclusively a TAC exercise, either. SAC sends bomber strikes in, sometimes to be met and escorted to a target by fighters, to augment the TAC tactical strike force. US Navy and US Marine squadrons send fighter and attack detachments to try out their techniques. AWACS aircraft will participate, controlling a friendly force. Tankers orbit the area, for added realism, as the fighters break out for refuelling just before entering the range area to fight.

It is the closest thing to war that it is possible to replicate, and the general improvement in the performance levels and skills of TAC's fighter pilots has begun to show.

There are other assignments for the command, such as reconnaissance, flown by a number of types including the new Lockheed TR-1, and the older RF-4C, Lockheed EC-130 and Boeing EC-135 types. TAC also commands the 1st Special Operations Wing, a unique organization that packs a number of strange skills into an elite trio of squadrons operating Lockheed AC-130H

*For the technical buffs the oblique white line on the fin of each of these Phantoms is an HF shunt aerial. That, and the dark camera window on the side of the nose, shows that these are RF-4C photo aircraft from the 363rd TRW, seen at Nellis during the 1981 'Red Flag' exercise.*

*A gaggle of A-7D-10 attack bombers, the first model to have the Allison/Rolls-Royce engine, during shakedown flying in the early 1970s. They caused many surprises with pinpoint bombing accuracy.*

*Afterburners in full cry, this Lockheed SR-71A lifts off the runway at Beale AFB, California.*

gunships, MC-130E search and rescue models (for which read insertion and recovery of agents), plus Sikorsky CH-3E, Sikorsky HH-53 and Bell UH-1N helicopters that can be arranged in a number of interesting configurations.

## Air National Guard and Air Force Reserve

A major portion of US Air Force strength is found in units of the Air National Guard and the Air Force Reserve. These units meet the same standards that are required of regular squadrons, and often now are flying the same equipment. It was not always so; ANG and AFR units used to be equipped with cast-offs from the regular squadrons as new aircraft entered TAC or SAC. But now, newer combat aircraft like the A-10A and A-7 Corsair II are joining ANG and AFR

# The United States Air Force

*Right: When the Reagan administration cancelled the new McDonnell Douglas C-17 in early 1982 it stated its intention to put the C-5 Galaxy back into production in an improved version called C-5N. Basically the world's most capable airlifter, the original C-5A version has from the start of its service, in December 1969, been dogged by structural problems.*

*Left: Lockheed's C-141 was lengthened with body plug inserts, and the C-141B was the result. Now earlier C-141A models are being converted. While they were at it, this experimental camouflage finish was tested. Note the use of counter-shading, with lighter colours in natural shadow areas tail and wing.*

squadrons. Increasingly, those squadrons are taking over missions that only recently were the province of the regular force. Professionalism is at a very high level in these reserve units; they participate in 'Red Flag' and other manoeuvres and exercises, and not infrequently make better scores in bombing and air combat than do their contemporaries in regular squadrons.

The cutting edge of USAF air power is concentrated in Tactical Air Command, and its new equipment and carefully polished pilot skills have increased its capabilities manyfold during the past few years. Now, TAC is settling back to the task of completing the conversion of its units to new aircraft, the passing along of its wisdom to successive classes of new pilots, and the continuing training that makes a fighter pilot and helps preserve him in the outnumbered combats he will be expected to win.

*Below: It takes a fair amount of piloting skill to spear that drogue from a helicopter, and all those blades are pretty close! Here, a Sikorsky HH-53 rescue helicopter refuels from a Lockheed HC-130P in Vietnam.*

# The Weapons of Air Combat

Aircraft are getting better all round, but they're really just becoming more sophisticated platforms for even better weapons. Major advances with active sensors attached to the weapons themselves multiply the effectiveness of their 'parent' aircraft beyond previous comprehension, and send shivers up the spines of would-be adversaries.

*A target aircraft meets its fiery fate at the hands of an air-launched missile. Any combat pilot can expect a short career in a real conflict.*

*By far the most expensive AAM in the West, the AIM-54 Phoenix can engage targets at a range of around 100 miles (161 km), about the same range as some fighter aircraft of earlier wars.*

In the beginning, there were 0.3-in (7.62-mm) machine-guns and—by today's standards—tiny bombs. There were many attempts to get the former to fire through the propeller disc, and to get the latter to drop cleanly from the crude bomb releases used in the later months of World War I. In early months, bombs often were dropped by hand over the side of the aeroplane.

Fighter kills were made by getting as close behind the enemy as possible before firing. Since the aircraft of that day were generally weak structurally, and not very stable aerodynamically, a good burst of machine-gun fire often did enough damage to the airframe itself to have it collapse, break apart or catch fire. It is likely, although data could never be assembled to prove it, that the majority of pilots shot down were not killed or even seriously wounded by gunfire, but had gone down alive in the wreckage of their broken biplanes.

World War II began with very similar armament, except that the synchronization problem had long since been solved, and the twin 0.3-in (7.62-mm) machine-guns that were standard

# The Weapons of Air Combat

*Left: As the air-to-air Genie rocket with warhead designed to carry a nuclear weapon drops from the open weapons bay of a General Dynamics F-106A, its rocket motor ignites with a brilliant flash.*

*Right: If any enemy ever gets this view of an F-15 he ought not to miss, because over 600 sq ft (55.7 m²) of wing is hardly a point target. What should stop him ever getting the chance are the APG-63 radar, four AIM-7F Sparrows and four AIM-9L Sidewinders.*

armament in September 1939 had better ballistic performance than those of November 1918. Heavier armament meant simply increasing the number of machine-guns (early Supermarine Spitfires mounted eight 0.303-in/7.7-mm Brownings) or mixing 0.3-in (7.62-mm) guns with 0.5-in (12.7-mm) guns, as was done on the first American fighters of that war. German and Japanese fighters appeared early in combat with 20-mm cannon, and British and American fighters later were equipped with cannon, often in a mix with 0.5-in (12.7-mm) guns or other armament.

But World War II introduced the potential for major change in fighter armament because of two innovations. The first was the unguided rocket, a weapon developed for ripple fire against formations of USAF bombers. The initial use of these by German interceptors had terrifying results and, had they become available earlier or in great quantity, they would have increased

*Below: This study of a 388th TFW F-16A clearly shows the difference in control-fin shape between the cropped double-delta AIM-9J series AAMs inboard and the long-span pointed AIM-9L AAMs on the tip shoes. Farther inboard are two 3,000-lb (1361-kg) M118 bombs, two 370-US gal (1401-litre) tanks and, on the centreline, an ALQ-131 ECM pod.*

# The Weapons of Air Combat

*A pair of Grumman A-6 Intruders drop sticks of bombs over South East Asia during the Vietnam war. The Intruder's advanced avionics marked a major improvement in the ability to lay down ordnance accurately in support of local ground forces in all weathers.*

the bomber loss rate substantially. The second was the air-launched guided missile, even in its crude form the portent of automatic death. The German use of these in limited air-to-surface bombing only hinted at what might come.

Paralleling these improvements in armament was a change in the operational use of fighter aircraft. As World War II wore on, and more and more fighters became available to the Allies and fewer to the Germans and Japanese, the classic role of the Allied fighter broadened. Increasingly they were assigned to attack and light bombing missions against ground targets such as bridges, marshalling yards, rail tunnels, oil storage facilities, ammunition dumps, airfields with reserve aircraft, and the like. They were performing the interdiction mission, and were doing it with bomb loads that were only somewhat smaller than those carried routinely by the Boeing B-17s and Consolidated B-24s classed as heavy bombers.

*A couple of bomb trailers carrying Mk 81 Snakeye high-drag bombs wait to be unloaded to arm an A-7A Corsair II of Attack Squadron 147 ('Argonauts'). The locale is probably NAS Lemoore, California.*

*Planned as a US Navy interceptor with Sparrow missiles, the F-4 was later laden with attack weapons, especially after it joined the US Air Force. Here an F-4D-29 (foreground) and F-4D-28 tote Paveway laser-homing 'smart bombs' during the Vietnam war.*

*Planned as a US Navy interceptor with Sparrow missiles, the F-4 was later laden with attack weapons, especially after it joined the US Air Force. Here an F-4D-29 (foreground) and F-4D-28 tote Paveway laser-homing 'smart bombs' during the Vietnam war.*

With heavier armament and the ability to carry 2,500 lb (1134 kg) or more of bombs, the fighter became a fighter-bomber. In Europe, it was Republic's P-47 Thunderbolt that made the change easily, becoming a superb ground attacker instead of the high-altitude fighter it had been designed to be. In the Pacific, the Lockheed P-38 Lightning assumed that attack role, combining its range, performance and carrying capability to good advantage. As a footnote, the P-38 performed nobly as a bomber in Europe, and was even sent in strength to bomb the refineries at Ploesti as part of the continuing attack on that production centre.

Today's fighters and fighter-bombers (the terms are almost entirely interchangeable now) can be armed with an astounding variety of weapons, the heritage of World War II armament and tactical developments.

An old principle of small cannon design was rediscovered and applied to the design of

*A Vought A-7 is seen here releasing a Walleye TV-guided bomb in a dive attack over mountainous territory. The digital nav-attack system of the A-7 brought a major advance in terrain avoidance and weapon-delivery accuracy.*

Though the 'Scooter' cannot lay down as many Snakeye high-drag bombs as can the A-6, the later models of A-4 can do so with accuracy in the 50-ft (15-m) class. These late A-4M Skyhawk IIs from VMA-223 ('Bulldogs') have every 'mod con' including double the previous amount of gun ammunition.

# The Weapons of Air Combat

modern aircraft cannon. The revolving barrels of the Gatling gun, a contemporary weapon available to General George A. Custer (but which he did not take with him to his last battle), became the basic layout for rapid-firing automatic aircraft cannon of both 20-mm and 30-mm size. These guns fire at rates between about 35 and 100 rounds per second, and a 2-second burst from either is enough to saw through any aircraft and most armoured vehicles. The 20-mm cannon has become the standard gun for air-to-air combat, and the 30-mm cannon is the weapon for anti-tank combat. Both those tasks demand a fairly close approach to the target before firing, and so cannon are defined as close-in weapons or, sometimes, dog-fighting weapons.

## Intercept weapons

A variety of air-to-air missiles is available to modern American combat aircraft, missiles that can be used at ranges from those encountered in dog-fighting to distances beyond visual range. The typical air combat missile arsenal includes: the AIM-4F/G Falcon, using semi-active radar homing, arming the F-106 interceptors of ADTAC; the AIM-9 Sidewinder, a family of missiles using infra-red homing, arming both US Navy and USAF fighters for the short-range engagement; the AIM-7 Sparrow, another family of missiles, using semi-active radar homing, covering

*Compared with the later models the austerely equipped early A-4 Skyhawks looked positively naked — though more aesthetically pleasing. This A-4E served in CVW-5 with a squadron now disbanded, VA-55, from USS Midway. What is of interest here is the AGM-12 Bullpup under the right wing, the first air-to-surface guided missile to go into service since some Luftwaffe ASMs in World War II.*

SAC tends to think in global terms, so perhaps its was not too extraordinary that Boeing's AGM-69A hypersonic defence-suppression missile should have been named SRAM (for Short-Range Attack Missile) even though it can fly over 100 miles (161 km). Sometimes SRAMs are carried on underwing pylons by the FB-111A, but this example has one on the left of its weapon bay, and a clean exterior to allow the full 655-mph (1055-kmh) low penetration speed.

When Boeing had to stretch the AGM-86A ALCM (Air-Launched Cruise Missile) to meet a requirement for greatly enhanced range the company produced a much better missile; but it no longer fits the rotary launcher in the B-52 (which was originally tailored to the SRAM). Eventually, late in the 1980s, the B-52G force may be modified to carry eight ALCMs internally, but at present they fit only on the inboard wing pylons. This special test drop from the internal bay was not representative of current SAC armament.

the medium-range engagement for both the US Navy and Air Force; and the AIM-54 Phoenix, a long-range missile with semi-active radar homing, now used only on the US Navy's F-14A for engagements beyond visual range.

During the Vietnam war, 'smart' bombs made their first appearance in combat. In contrast to 'iron' or 'dumb' bombs, which follow only a free-fall ballistic trajectory after release, 'smart' bombs have some sort of guidance mechanism, generally a laser head, that enables a remote operator to adjust the trajectory of the bomb for pinpoint precision. Further, they have additional fin area to increase the lift and so extend their normal trajectory. Smart bombs also use infra-red or electro-optical seekers, and are classified under the broad category of HOBOS (Homing Bomb System). The most sophisticated of these is the Walleye guided bomb, used in Vietnam and currently available for fighter-bomber armament. It is guided by television and

# The Weapons of Air Combat

*Possibly built in larger numbers than any other precision-guided missile, TOW is by far the commonest anti-tank missile of US forces and of many allied nations. Here the guidance operator in the Cobra front cockpit is glued to his sight.*

has considerably better glide range than an equivalent free-fall weapon because of a large cruciform lifting surface.

Glide bombs, like the Walleye, are decendants of similar, but crude, weapons employed during World War II. In their most recent form, as the USAF's GBU-15, they exhibit a degree of aerodynamic modernity and bombing accuracy that was unavailable to earlier weapons designers. The GBU-15 family is built around about a ton of explosives contained in a 12-ft (3.66-m) long body equipped with a set of wings and tail surfaces. It is a modular design, enabling field assembly, and it comes in two basic forms, one for a moderate extension of the free-fall range and the other for a substantial extension.

Other air-to-surface missiles in the current armoury include the Shrike AGM-45A/B and HARM AGM-88A anti-radiation missiles. These clever weapons arm the 'Wild Weasel' hunter-

*A basic requirement for the F-18 Hornet was compatability with the medium-range Sparrow AAM (which at present is not carried by the F-16). Hughes provided the APG-65 digital multi-mode radar, and here a Sparrow streaks on its way from the seventh development Hornet during missile trials at Point Mugu.*

*At 6,000 rounds per minute, this General Dynamics F-16 Fighting Falcon will get through its stock of 515 shells in five seconds! Its M61A-1 20-mm Vulcan 'Gatling gun' is equally useful for both air-to-ground strafing and air-to-air combat.*

# The Weapons of Air Combat

killer teams that seek out and destroy enemy missile batteries. The missiles use a passive radar guidance system, and ride the beam projected by enemy radar back to its source, with satisfying results. Shrike was used during the Vietnam war and now is being replaced by the higher-speed HARM (High-velocity Anti-Radiation Missile).

Of similar size to the GBU-15 family is the US Navy's AGM-84A Harpoon, although it weighs in at less than half that of the GBU-15. It is an anti-shipping missile, with an active radar seeker, and is available to arm US Navy and US Marine Corps attack aircraft.

All the services use one form or another of the air-to-surface AGM-65 Maverick, 450 lb (204 kg) worth of explosive, guidance and rocket propulsion. It is available with a variety of guidance heads, including passive laser, television, and imaging infra-red seekers.

Even with these new categories of missiles, there remains a huge armoury of demolition and chemical bombs, unguided rockets that are a prime weapon for the US Army's gunship helicopters, aerial mines laid by fighter-bombers or bombers, depth bombs, incendiaries like napalm (still a most effective weapon of area destruction), and fragmentation and cluster bombs. The latter are the kinds of munitions being developed specifically to stop an armoured advance.

## Anti-Armor weapons

Under the programme designation of WAAM (Wide Area Anti-Armor Munitions), the US Air Force is hoping to develop a cluster bomb with unique properties. The bomb explodes with energy to melt its own fragments. As they streak through the air in molten form, aerodynamic forces shape them into streamlined bodies, forms with much lower drag and thus capable of maintaining their high speed for a much longer time. That adds up to greatly improved penetration characteristics, and a deadly rain against armoured vehicles. Until WAAM and its derivatives are available, earlier cluster munitions with wide-area dispersions are the weapons of choice against broad columns of armour.

There is a remarkable ingenuity that goes into the conception and development of these unusual weapons of war. Self-contained rudimentary intelligence systems steer bombs and missiles, seek out and lock on to targets that emit heat or return radiation. A miniature smelting and forging operation flies through the air, processing crude lumps of metal into streamlined shapes. And, separated in thousands of warheads in underground bunkers, are lumps of radioactive material that only need to be brought together rapidly to produce a blast with heat emissions that rival that of a sun, and radiation that can kill at distances of tens of miles.

*It does fit: you have to hump it a little bit, and into the drum go 1,350 rounds of 30-mm ammunition to feed the voracious appetite of the GAU-8 cannon that can spew 4,000 rounds per minute. That's 20 seconds of firing there.*